A Brief History of the Olympic Games

D1336357

Please return/renew this item by the last date shown. Books may also be renewed by phone or Internet.

Hertfordshire

From Area codes 01923 or 020:
Renewals: 01923 471373   Textphone: 01923 471599
From the rest of Herts:
Renewals: 01438 737373 Textphone: 01438 737599
www.hertsdirect.org/libraries

Brief Histories of the Ancient World

This new series offers concise, accessible, and lively accounts of central aspects of the ancient world. Each book is written by an acknowledged expert in the field and provides a compelling overview, for readers new to the subject and specialists alike.

Published
A Brief History of the Olympic Games
David C. Young

In Preparation
A Brief History of Astrology
Roger Beck

A Brief History of Oracles, Divination, and Prophecy
Sarah Iles Johnston

A Brief History of the Olympic Games

David C. Young

Blackwell Publishing

BLACKWELL PUBLISHING
350 Main Street, Malden, MA 02148–5020, USA
108 Cowley Road, Oxford OX4 1JF, UK
550 Swanston Street, Carlton, Victoria 3053, Australia

First published 2004 by Blackwell Publishing Ltd

Library of Congress Cataloging-in-Publication Data
Young, David C.
  A brief history of the Olympic games / David C. Young.
    p. cm. — (Brief histories of the ancient world)
  Includes bibliographical references and index.
  ISBN 1-4051-1129-1 (alk. paper) – ISBN 1-4051-1130-5 (alk. paper)
  1. Olympic games (Ancient)–History. I. Title. II. Series.
  GV23.Y68 2004
  796.48—dc22

                                                    2004001156

A catalogue record for this title is available from the British Library.

Set in 10/13pt Galliard
by Graphicraft Ltd, Hong Kong
Printed and bound in the United Kingdom
by TJ International Ltd, Padstow, Cornwall

The publisher's policy is to use permanent paper from mills that operate a sustainable forestry policy, and which has been manufactured from pulp processed using acid-free and elementary chlorine-free practices. Furthermore, the publisher ensures that the text paper and cover board used have met acceptable environmental accreditation standards.

For further information on
Blackwell Publishing, visit our website:
http://www.blackwellpublishing.com

Iphitos established the Olympic Games, since the citizens of Elis were very pious. Because of such things, these men prospered. While the other cities were always at war with one another, these people enjoyed a general peace, not only for themselves, but also for visitors, with a result that here, of all places, an especially great number of people assembled.

Strabo, *Geography* 8.3.33

For Juju

Contents

Figures

Preface

The Olympic Games. Few phrases immediately bring to mind so many images – grandeur, excellence, internationalism, history – maybe even a glimmer of peace. True, a few images are negative. But for many of us the positive images so outweigh them that even real flaws in the games seem almost negligible. A fan of the Olympics since boyhood, for more than twenty years I have spent much of my time doing research on the ancient Olympics and the early years of the modern revival. I therefore welcomed the chance to write this book.

In my *Olympic Myth of Greek Amateur Athletics* (1984) I argued that the ancient Greeks did not know or practice the concept of an amateur athlete. At that time most classicists, sport historians, and the media still believed that the ancient Olympics were "strictly amateur," to use the phrase of Avery Brundage. Brundage, as president of the International Olympic Committee, cited the precedent of ancient Greece to justify his enforcing the strictest of amateur rules. Brundage's departure, more than my book, hastened the disappearance of amateurism from the modern Olympic Games. But nowadays virtually no classicist or historian would attribute amateurism to the ancient Greeks. Amateurism, the bane of the modern Olympics for almost a hundred years, is now nothing but a relic of history in classical scholarship, as well.

This research led me to wonder about the origins of the modern Olympic Games. I had read a 1930 book, written in Greek, which recounted a series of modern Greek Olympiads that began in 1859. Yet all other histories said that the earliest suggestion of holding modern Olympics was made in Paris in 1894 by Pierre de Coubertin, who then almost single-handedly produced the very first modern Olympics at Athens in 1896. On a tip from Stephen Miller, I found a wealth of information on those pre-1896 Athens Olympics in the papers of Stephanos Dragoumis, president of the Greek Olympic Committee in the late nineteenth century.

These papers, recently willed to an Athens library, contained not only information on these earlier Greek games, but also letters from Coubertin and from the Englishman W. P. Brookes. In 1987 I published an extraordinary letter written by Brookes which I found in the Dragoumis papers. Soon I received correspondence from two scholars in Köln, whose students had been researching the papers of Dr. Brookes in England. When I myself studied those papers, I soon realized that – when combined with the Dragoumis documents in Athens – they uncovered a wholly new and different story of how our own Olympics began.

The modern revival was a slow process wherein a few Greeks and Dr. Brookes advocated the idea of an Olympic revival for decades, but never fully succeeded. A sporadic series of modern revivals in each country attracted little interest or support. Yet after the aging Brookes told the young Frenchman of their efforts, Coubertin achieved what they had not.

With the indispensable cooperation of the gentlemen in Köln, Professors W. Decker and J. Rühl and their students, I wrote the story which these documents revealed. The result was my *The Modern Olympics: A Struggle for Revival* (1996).

Al Bertrand of Blackwell Publishing read my two Olympics books and invited me to write this *Brief History of the Olympic Games* for the new series, Brief Histories of the Ancient World. Since I am a classicist, my interest and studies in the ancient games never faltered while I was concentrating on the modern games. I accepted Mr. Bertrand's invitation, knowing that there was a great need for a book such as this. Bertrand also suggested that I end the book with a chapter summarizing my research on how the modern Olympics began. As I wrote, I had mainly in mind the interested general reader and college students in classes on the Olympics or ancient sport. For these readers there has been no accessible and comprehensive work on this subject. Yet I hope sport historians and classical colleagues will find the book useful, as well.

For proper names that are generally familiar or frequent in Olympic histories I use the English versions as adapted from Latin: Thucydides, Aeschylus, and Plato, rather than the exact transliteration of the Greek (Thoukydides, Aischylos, Platon). Less familiar names appear spelled more like the original Greek: Akousilaos rather than Acusilaus, Ikkos rather than Iccus. Citations of the standard Greek authors, by universal custom, are given in Latin: Lucian rather than Loukianos.

For truly obscure sources, I sometimes cite a secondary source as well as, or instead of, the primary one. For example, when I quote Brookes' statement on rare plants (p. 187, below), I cite the passage where I reproduced it in my own 1996 book, not the elusive original article in an 1876 Shropshire newspaper. Such items as the series Oxyrhynchus Papyri are likely to be found in most major university libraries, but are not user-friendly for non-classicists. I therefore cite Harris' translation, as well as the original papyrus publication in Greek (p. 119, below). Sometimes, if the original source would be generally unavailable to most readers and what I say could not be controversial to classical scholars, I omit the source.

I thank Mihaela Lipetz-Penes of the Romanian Olympic Committee (and Olympic gold medalist, javelin, Tokyo, 1964) for taking me to examine and photograph Zappas' Romanian tomb. I thank Paul Zappas of Los Angeles for sending me photos of the Albanian tomb, which he took on a difficult journey to find it in the remote, tiny village of Labova.

To publish with the help of the staff at Blackwell has been an unusual pleasure. I start with Al Bertrand, who first suggested that I write this book, and provided his valuable judgment and suggestions along the way. I thank most of all Angela Cohen. She guided the book through all stages of writing and production, always quickly replying to any query, giving me needed technical judgments or information. Jack Messenger is every author's dream of a copy editor. He let me keep my sentences, without compelling me to publish his. I thank Ed Barton for preparing the index. My greatest debt is to Dr. Judy Ann Turner, an ancient historian and my wife.

Without her support and her tolerating my late nights, I could never have finished. And, as usual, as a critic of my writing and research, she was the closest thing to quality control that I could have.

1

Introduction

Rhodon: "Maybe he will really do it!" Tryphon: "No, he won't. He can't. Nobody could ever do that. Look how far behind he is. He is still way behind." Rhodon: "Yes, but he's gaining on him fast. Look, he's getting ready to pass him. He *is* passing him! Unbelievable!" Tryphon: "You were right. Look at that finish kick! He *is* going to do it. I don't believe it! He won! He really did it." Rhodon: "Well, he always was the only one who thought he could. By Zeus, what a runner!" Tryphon: "There has never been another like him. Never, *in all these centuries*! He is the greatest runner ever, in all history."

That conversation itself is imaginary; for it is set in the summer of 69 AD. But it is not groundless. Some very similar conversation indeed took place among the spectators at the stadium track at Olympia that August day. And all the characters are real. "He" is a young runner named Polites, from Caria, a place now in south-western Turkey. "It" is to win the long distance race at the Olympic Games that day. That victory in itself is hardly remarkable. Someone had won that race every four years for centuries. These two spectators are so astonished at Polites' victory because he had already won the shortest sprint, the *stade*, about 200 meters, earlier that same day.[1] Tryphon and Rhodon knew something about running. They were the winners of the *stade* in the previous and the following Olympiads, respectively. Polites won that shortest race *and* the longest race. That feat no one – in more than 800 years of

Olympic competition – had ever achieved before – nor did anyone after him. And no modern Olympic athlete has ever won both a long distance race and a short sprint, to say nothing of winning both on the same day.

In the Atlanta Olympics of 1996 Michael Johnson became the first person ever to win both the 200 meter race and the 400. He himself proudly proclaimed he had "made history," and his unique double Olympic victory was celebrated as one of the greatest athletic accomplishments of all time (*Runners World*, November 1996). It had never been done before – at least not in the modern Olympics. In antiquity, at least a dozen athletes had combined those two victories before Polites, who himself had already performed that 200 and 400 double earlier the same day. But the 400 has never been classed as a distance race. It is barely a "middle distance" event.

To win both the shortest sprint and such a distance race more than two miles long at the same Olympiad is a nearly incredible achievement. No modern runner has ever been so versatile. The long and short distances require, our coaches believe, very different kinds of runners and training. The proper type of muscle fibers, breathing, training, and technique for the two styles of running are wholly different. Polites' diversity at running seemed truly exceptional in antiquity, too. Pausanias (second century AD) calls it "a great marvel," and adds that Polites could switch from the distance style to sprinting in a very brief time. His "finishing kick" in the distance race must have been something special to see.

Appreciation of Polites' deed increases all the more if we put it in its full context, "all those centuries." The ancient Olympics spanned more than a millennium, from about 776 BC to approximately 400 AD. They were eight centuries old before any Polites emerged, and they continued for several more centuries without ever seeing another like him. He is truly unique. But the nature of Greek record keeping combined with those 800 years almost compelled him, if he wished to achieve anything remarkable, to try to do what he did (see chapter 3). The failure of any modern Olympian so far to equal Polites' unique double is understandable, almost even inevitable. Our modern games are scarcely more than a century old. Perhaps in seven hundred or so more years, a runner like Polites will dazzle some distant future generation.

It is not irrelevant or even badly anachronistic to compare ancient runners to our own. There are no others to compare them with. In all of the world's history our athletic system is the only one at all similar to the Greeks'. The modern world seems almost sports-mad, with large portions of the media entirely devoted to sport. In financial terms, it is one of our biggest industries. No other culture has ever had nearly so strong an interest in so widespread an athletic system as ours. Because of modern communication and globalization, even ancient Greece is barely comparable. But in its attention to athletics and in the cultural role they played, by far the closest to us was ancient Greece, from which our own system of sport has, in fact, borrowed most heavily.

Why was competitive sport in antiquity found in Greece, and not elsewhere? Early in the last century the noted scholar Jakob Burckhardt argued that there was something special in the Greek national character that drove them to a unique competitive spirit. It is true that Attic dramas, both tragedy and comedy, were parts of prize competitions. Musicians, too, often competed for prizes, some-times in the same festivals as the athletes. Plato even calls musicians in such contexts "athletes"; for that word merely means "competi-tor for a prize" (*Laws* 764D).

For nearly a century Burckhardt's argument that the Greeks were uniquely competitive received wide acceptance (Gardiner 1930: 1–2). Recently, however, some of the best scholars have disagreed. They argue that the earlier cultures of the ancient Near East and Egypt had sport as well, and stress their strong and sweeping influ-ence on Greece in other matters.

Yet depictions of wrestling bouts or other combative contests in these other cultures offer no proof that these activities were part of a larger or formal competition. And they do not tell us who the competitors were or why they are competing. They are merely pictures of men wrestling or fighting. In Egypt and elsewhere the rulers (or others in honor of the rulers) indeed hunted animals and engaged in other physical activities. But none of these things any-where seems to have influenced or resembled the Greek athletic meeting. I join many others who think that Burckhardt's thesis still survives a thorough examination rather well (Golden 1998: 30–3; Poliakoff 1987: 104–11; Scanlon 2002: 9–10).

In speaking of Greek athletics we should avoid the word "sports." Greek athletics have little or nothing to do with sport or games. While some of the events were sometimes practiced for recreation, the festivals, at least, were far from being a diversion. No word ever associated with them could translate as anything like "sport." And there were no contests at all for teams, not even a relay race. The only events were for individuals. The Greeks had team games, even team ball games, but they played no part in athletic festivals such as the Olympics.

The term "Olympic Games" is itself a bad mistranslation of Greek *Olympiakoi agones*. That error results from the intervening Latin words, *ludus*, *ludi*, and *ludicrum*, which *do*, in fact, connote sport and games. Our word "ludicrous" comes from there.[2] The Romans did not take Greek athletics seriously. But the Greek word *agones* can never refer to "games." Rather, it means "struggles" or "contests"; or even "pains." Our word "agony" derives from it. The word "play," as well, has no application at all to Greek athletics. The Greek word for "play," *paizein*, comes from the word *pais*, "child." It can be used when adults play music, board games and even ball games, but never for any event in Greek athletics.

Our own athletic sports, in the main, developed from children's games, play, passed on to adults through the schools. Few people realize that athletics, as we know them, are a rather recent addition to our own culture. Even 150 years ago, other than some rowing and cricket contests restricted to England, there were practically no athletic sports anywhere in the world. By the middle of the nineteenth century, English schoolboys were developing some ball games and other contests. The schoolboys eventually took these activities with them into the colleges and universities, where more formal rules and procedures were established. The original nucleus and still the mainstay of our Olympics, the track and field sports (called simply "athletics" outside of America), arose mainly from a conscious imitation of ancient Greek practices. Some early Olympic revivals in Britain and modern Greece, as well as the activities of English students, contributed to this imitation and the promotion of these contests (see chapter 13). From England, track and field athletics and many other sports spread first to nineteenth-century America, then to Europe, and eventually to all corners of the world (Guttmann 1978: 57).

With a few obvious exceptions such as golf, tennis, and base-ball, it is readily apparent that even professional sports in America descended from college activities: the professional offspring has never fully separated from the collegiate sire. Generally, then, in our society most sports find their eventual ancestry in children's games. And baseball's origin in child's play is especially obvious when we say "play ball" where the phrase is historically most apt.

In ancient Greece, however, athletics were first and foremost an activity for grown men. The events themselves might have had a prehistoric origin in ordinary play among boys. In any culture and time a group of boys with leisure will naturally test such questions as who can jump or throw a stone the farthest. Who can wrestle another to the ground? Who can run to the end of the field first? But the Greeks differed from other ancient and more recent cultures in making resolutions to these questions a serious activity for grown men. Even at the beginning they did not, as other peoples have done, relegate them to the inconsequential world of children. Formal competitions for adult men existed for many years before there were any formal competitions for boys. *When Greek boys competed in athletics, they were acting like men, not the reverse, as in other cultures.*

Romans, even when they sponsored Greek-style athletic festivals, never themselves participated in them. And when we read of grown men in Persia contesting for prizes (*athla*), the prizes were set for whatever company of soldiers could best perform military drills in perfect unison, "like a chorus," so that no individual would stand out (Xenophon, *Cyropaedia* 1.2.12; 1.6.18). The Greek goal was the opposite; namely, to be the one who stands out, to be, as Pindar puts it, the one who is "separated out from the other athletes," literally "distinguished," to be the best of all (*Nemean* 7.7–8). Greek athletics were always, in principle, the pursuit of individual excellence.

Athletics in Homer

In general, the principle which Pindar expresses was true from the outset of recorded Greek thought, even in Homer, where study of Greek thought must begin. In the *Iliad* the explicit driving force behind Homer's hero, Achilles, is to be – and to be known as –

"the best of the Achaeans" ("Achaeans" is Homer's word for the Greeks). It is not surprising that the grown men in such a culture participate in athletic competitions, seize an occasion to stand out from the rest of the crowd.

Homer does not mention Olympic Games, a sure anachronism; but he is certainly familiar with athletic contests. Already in his day the Olympics may well have been the most prominent among them. Homer's heroes of the Trojan War indeed participate in athletics. As his best friend Patroclus lies dead and unburied, Achilles decides that the most appropriate way to honor him would be to hold an athletic meeting and distribution of *athla*, prizes (*Iliad* 23.256–897). He sets up the most valuable prizes for the chariot race, which takes place first on the program. In a unique passage, Idomeneus offers to make a bet with Ajax on the outcome of the race. As the two argue, Achilles stops their wrangling and never again in Greek literature does anyone allude to the subject of athletic betting. Diomedes, known for his ability with horses, wins.

The second event is boxing. Although he himself admits that he is a poor warrior and of little use on the battlefield, Epeios claims he is the best boxer. So he is, as he readily knocks out the only contender. A common theory about Greek athletics finds their origin and purpose in military training. Yet in Homer the best boxer is a poor soldier. Moreover, some highly successful generals of the Classical period thought athletics were detrimental to military training. The fourth century BC general Epaminondas of Thebes discouraged his men from athletics. In the next century, the military mastermind Philopoemen actually forbade his troops to do any athletics at all (Plutarch, *Moralia* 192c–d, 788a; *Philopoemen* 3.2–4). The military theory has little to commend it.

Next is the wrestling match. Ajax and Odysseus, major figures in the *Iliad*, square off upright in a preliminary hold. They are evenly matched. Each has gained one throw when Achilles calls the bout a draw. The only foot race at these games is the *diaulos*, down the course once and back. Later, at least, the *diaulos* was about 400 meters. Here Odysseus need not share first place, because Athena – who always seems there to give Odysseus special protection and help – trips the only man running in front of her favorite before they reach the finish line.

There are four more events on Achilles' program: (1) a kind of fencing with swords; (2) a weight throw; (3) archery; and (4) a spear throw. Neither archery nor fencing was ever on the Olympic program. The weight thrown in the *Iliad*, called a *solos*, seems to be a very large, perhaps shapeless chuck of iron, nothing like a discus. The spear throw event is not actually held, since when it is announced, everyone defers to Agamemnon's known ability there. But the javelin throw was a regular part of Olympic competition.

Another athletic contest takes place in Homer's *Odyssey* (8.100–214). The account here is shorter, but contains much of interest. In the course of his long odyssey seeking to return home after the Trojan War, Odysseus suffers many mishaps. Once he is shipwrecked and washes up on the shore of a strange and unknown island inhabited by very hospitable people called Phaeacians. They are a peaceful, seafaring people who do a good deal of feasting, singing, and dancing. They treat the marooned Greek sailor with every kindness, and even hold a feast in his honor. After a bard has entertained everyone, the king suggests that they hold a set of athletic contests (*athla*).

The young men of Phaeacia compete in boxing, wrestling, a foot race, long jump, and discus throw. The weight thrown here is explicitly a real athletic discus, not a lump of iron. At that point, Laodamas, son of the Phaeacian king, asks Odysseus if he wishes to compete in any of the contests. His invitation ends with some memorable words:

> So long as a man lives, he has no greater glory
> than what he wins with his feet or his hands in the games.

At first Odysseus declines to compete. But then a brash youth starts to taunt him, suggesting that Odysseus probably does not know the "many athletic events that men have." He points to Odysseus' sea-beaten body and suggests that he looks like a merchant. "You don't look like any athlete." More than a little miffed, Odysseus takes up the challenge and the largest discus in the heap. He then lets fly what seems to be a new Phaeacian discus record, far surpassing all earlier marks. He then offers to fight any of them in boxing. No one accepts the challenge

Thus as our Western literary tradition starts with Homer, so does the study of Greek athletics, with these two extensive narratives of athletic contests, one in each poem. The characters and events in Homer obviously fall into the realm of myth rather than history. But Heinrich Schliemann (1822–90) did not believe that. He thought Homer's tale of a Trojan War was true. In the latter nineteenth century he found and excavated first Troy, in northwestern Turkey, then Mycenae in southern Greece. In Homer, Agamemnon, who organized and led the Greek army against Troy, was the king of Mycenae. Schliemann's excavations uncovered a surprisingly sophisticated late Bronze Age civilization which archaeologists still mine all around the Greek world. He called it "Mycenaean," sure that he had unearthed the remains of the civilization which Homer describes in his stories about the Trojan War. We now know that many of Schliemann's claims were false and too grandiose. Yet no one doubts the reality of Mycenaean civilization, or its relevance to the interpretation of Homer.

The difficult question is how much in Homer is an authentic memory of Mycenaean times, and how much comes from life in eighth-century Greece. That is the period in which scholars agree that the two poems, in the main, were composed. Do the athletic scenes in Homer tell us that such contests existed in Mycenaean times? Those very events? Wrestling and boxing are well attested in both the Mycenaean period and the historical Olympics, but they have no doubt existed in some form in most civilizations. The archery and fencing which occur in the *Iliad* were never held in the Olympics, but Homer may well have thought that they seemed appropriate in the military context of the Trojan War and those earlier days. Otherwise, every event listed in the *Iliad* and *Odyssey* was actually part of the regular Olympic program. There is, I think, cogent evidence that Homer, rather than preserving a memory of athletics centuries earlier, represents athletics in his own time. No discuses have turned up at Mycenae, and I am confident that they never will.

Scattered throughout the Homeric poems are recurrent references to athletic competition, enough of them to leave no doubt but that various kinds of athletic contests were a regular part of Homer's world. Homer is known for his many similes. In these similes, he uses the present tense and unquestionably refers to matters of his own day. When Achilles pursues Hector around the city of Troy, Homer says that they ran very fast: "For they were not competing for a sacrificial animal or an ox-hide, such as are the prizes in foot races. Hector's life was the stake. As prize-winning horses quickly make the turns, when a large prize is set, such as a tripod or a woman, when a man has died, so they ran around the city" (*Iliad* 22.159–66). Here is evidence for two distinct types of contests in the poet's own culture. First, Homer knows funeral games like the games for Patroclus recounted above. Athletic contests associated with funerals appear a number of times in early texts. Hesiod, probably Homer's younger contemporary, speaks of games he attended at the funeral of a man named Amphidamas, whose sons offered "many prizes" (*Works and Days* 631–40). Homer's heroes sometimes mention funeral games. Nestor, the old man of the Greek army, boasts about his success at funeral games for a man named Amarynkeas (*Iliad* 23.60–1). Funeral games continued in historical and Classical times (Roller 1981: 1–18).

Second, the mythical games at Phaeacia suggest that actual athletic contests were not limited to funerals even in Homer's society. There were other kinds. The prize of a sacrificial victim or hide almost certainly implies contests held in conjunction with a religious festival or rite, such as occurred on a much grander scale at Olympia (*Iliad* 22.159–66, above). Hesiod says that the goddess Hekate gives help "when men are competing for prizes at a contest. And when someone gains victory with his mighty strength he happily carries his fine prize home, and brings glory to his parents" (*Theogony* 435–8).

The spirit of athletic competition, then, and athletic contests themselves, were ingrained in the fabric of the Greek society which Homer himself knew. But when, we must ask, precisely did "Homer himself" live? Even here, howsoever briefly, we must broach what for centuries is the knottiest problem in Classical studies, called "the Homeric problem"; namely, whether the *Iliad* is the work of a single man, a kind of committee, or somewhere in between. "How do we get a text of Homer," we must ask, "when it seems that writing was at best embryonic when the poems were composed?" I summarize what most classicists generally believe.

Homer did not write down his poems; rather, he composed them orally. The approximate date most likely is about 725 BC. It is likely that the general product which we call the *Iliad* is the work of one man. That man, probably named Homer, combined as he wished a vast repertoire of oral poetry which had been developed and passed down by generations of poets before him. It is about this time, too, 725 BC, that we find the earliest evidence for writing in what later became the standard Greek alphabet. That writing system imported Semitic writing characters and changed them to render Greek sound values. The Olympic Games almost certainly began *before* that 725 date, and I think the athletics which Homer represents give us a good notion of what the early Olympics probably were like.

The painter of a well-known ancient vase, Sophilos, saw such a connection, too, it seems. He paints a scene labeled "Funeral games of Patroclus," which shows a hippodrome and stadium (figure 1.1). In the hippodrome a chariot race is taking place. Both it and the stadium are replete with ascending rows of seats, which look like some kind of bleachers and are occupied by cheering spectators, presumably the Greek army. The part of the vase showing the action in the stadium is broken off, but surely depicted some combative, athletic, or running event. The spectators on the right-hand seats could not be watching anything else.

One cannot imagine, even as mythology, such an athletic facility suddenly sprouting up, fully built, bleachers and all, near the Greeks' ships on the Trojan plain – just waiting there for the Greeks to have an athletic meeting. There is no hint of a stadium or hippodrome at the games in the *Iliad*. The artist cannot be portraying what Homer describes. Rather, he must depict what he himself knows.

Experts date the vase very early, about 580 BC or slightly later. At so early a date, only one site is possible to be known, and that is Olympia.[3] Sophilos' picture shows the stadium and hippodrome side by side, separated only by a tall embankment. That is how they were positioned at Olympia. Historians sometimes remark on Olympia's lack of seating, even after seating had been installed at other venues, almost as if the want of seating fits Olympia's reputation for conservatism and austerity (Sinn 2000: 73; Gardiner 1930: 252; Harris 1972: 57).

Figure 1.1 Funeral games of Patroclus, National Museum, Athens 15499, fragment of b.f. Attic mixing vessel painted by Sophilos, about 580 BC or soon thereafter

The unmistakable seating on the vase by Sophilos might appear to be an obstacle in seeing a reflection of Olympia there. But if rows of seats were merely cut into the terrain in a kind of terrace formation, there would of course be no trace remaining. Even wooden bleachers might leave nothing identifiable now. If not Olympia, the scene on the vase is enigmatic almost beyond belief. Surely no one will argue that the actual scene is on the plain of Troy; or that Sophilos was able to foretell what the setting of a future athletic festival would look like without ever knowing one.

2

Beginnings and Evidence

The Beginnings

The poet Pindar said that the games at Olympia eclipse all other
athletic contests as the sun eclipses the other stars in the daytime
sky (*Olympian* 1.1–7; see chapter 6, below). The Olympics were
the oldest of many Greek festivals, and by universal agreement, the
best. There is little certain about the details of the festival's origin,
how the competitions actually began. Greeks gave several rather
incompatible foundation legends; most are obviously pure myth.
I relate only the version given by Pindar, for it is first and foremost,
and Pindar occupies a preeminent position among Greek poets.
He attributes the founding of the games to one of the best-known
heroes of Greek myth, Herakles.

One of Herakles' labors was to cleanse the stables of Augeas,
which he did by diverting a river through them. When Augeas
refuses to pay, Herakles kills him and pillages his land, removing the
spoils to Pisa, a town adjacent to Olympia. Here is Pindar's tale:

> Then Zeus' mighty son assembled his entire army and all the booty at
>   Pisa. He marked out a sacred precinct for his father, the Altis,
> which he fenced in and set apart in the open. The plain around
> he turned into an area for feasts, and honored the river Alpheus.
> Herakles took out the best of the spoils and made an offering with
>   them,

and he established a quadrennial festival and contests for prizes,
the first Olympiad. Who then won the new crown
with his feet, hands, or chariot? Oionos the son of Likymnios
was best with his feet at running the straightway of the stade race.

Pindar then lists the winners at these first Olympics in wrestling, boxing, chariot race, javelin, and discus. He concludes his account of the Olympic beginnings: "Then the face of the moon with its lovely light shined on the evening, and the whole sanctuary resounded with song and festal joy in the mode of victory celebration."

I pass quickly over several lesser Olympic origin myths. But there was one tale of the festival's beginnings which is perhaps not wholly mythical. Olympia lay in the land of the Triphylians, "The three tribes." They belonged to the peoples of Arcadia, the very mountainous section of the central Peloponnesus. Their main city was Pisa, not far from the site itself, and Triphylians probably had control of the site in the earliest years. But they had to contend with the people of Elis, to the north, who at some early point took control from them. With only a few interruptions, the Eleans thereafter administered the site and organized the Olympic Games. Some scholars even accuse the Eleans of inventing legends in order to legitimize their claims to be the original sponsors of the games. Pausanias (second century BC) recounts the story which they apparently told to justify their authority. The king of Elis, Iphitos, was once instructed by the Delphic oracle to "restore the Olympics." He made a pact with the Spartan lawgiver, Lycurgus, and the Pisatan king, Cleomenes, to hold the games and to declare the thirty day Olympic truce, the *ekecheiria* which protected those going to the games. Pausanias saw an ancient discus with some writing on it which was purported to be the original product of this agreement. But the style of the letters which he says were inscribed on it proves that it could not be so old as the time Iphitos was said to live (5.20.1).

The site of Olympia lies in the valley of the River Alpheus in the northwestern Peloponnesus, about 15 kilometers inland from the west coast, where the rushing river exits into the sea. The valley is bounded on both sides by gentle hills. Northeast of the site is a larger hill, called the Hill of Cronus, the most distinctive landmark of the area. Olympia itself was never an inhabited town or city; it was from its start a religious precinct dedicated to the cult of Zeus. Over the years various structures were built on the grounds. The only permanent residents were some priests, although many thronged to it every four years and it was constantly visited by worshippers and tourists.

The "Altis," as Pindar calls it (above), local dialect for *alsos*, meant "Sacred Place," usually "Sacred Grove," because Greeks tended to place their sanctuaries in shady, well-wooded areas. The religious portion of the site, at Olympia always called by the name Altis, was clearly marked off from the secular grounds nearby, such as the stadium, any accommodations, baths, and other areas which served the tourists or the athletes more than the god.

When the religious cult was finally halted about 400 AD, Christians rather briefly occupied the site, even the Altis, until sometime in the sixth century. But then natural disasters, foreign invasions, and population shifts left it uninhabited and unattended throughout the Middle Ages and even beyond. In Europe, at least, Olympia was wholly forgotten for a millennium.

When the first printed editions of Pausanias and Pindar appeared in the early sixteenth century, they awakened the name of Olympia again. In 1667, John Milton briefly mentioned "Olympian Games" in *Paradise Lost*. The site itself, however, was still entirely buried, ignored, and unmarked. In 1723 the French Classical scholar Bernhard Montfaucon remarked that there must be important artifacts and unexplored ruins where ancient Olympia once was, and even suggested that someone should investigate it. A few travelers later did visit the site, and identified the temple of Zeus. But it was not until 1829, a full century after Montfaucon, that a French team undertook the very first excavations, mostly just in the temple of Zeus. This project was abandoned before it had accomplished much, and the site still awaited serious study.

Ernst Curtius, who had been interested in Olympia for decades, led a German team in the first systematic excavations in 1875, and a series of German archaeologists have carried on there intermittently until the present day. That group of distinguished excavators includes Schliemann's protégé, Dörpfeld, and most recently, Alfred

Mallwitz and Ulrich Sinn. The whole plan and chronology of the sanctuary is now well known. Progress at the site continues, mainly in materials from the Roman Empire.

While Bronze Age evidence at the site and surrounding plain is not wholly absent, the area was not, as some once thought, a cult center in Mycenaean times. But in the tenth, ninth, and eighth centuries, people brought thousands of animal figurines, especially cattle, but also horses and rams, to the site in various offerings. The deity honored seems to have been Zeus from the start, although early in Olympia's history there was built a separate altar to Gaia, Earth, on a rise at the foot of the Hill of Cronus. On the north, the River Cladeus raced down through the western part to join the Alpheus. But about 700 BC the Cladeus was redirected farther to the west, to give more room for the buildings and grounds of the sanctuary. Perhaps the first permanent item on the site was the altar of Zeus, which was tended regularly with sacrifices of animals, whose charred bones built up into a solid structure. This altar remained the focal point of the sanctuary for all the remaining centuries, and by Pausanias' time it towered above the visitors. Near it was the tomb of the hero Pelops, who gave his name to the entire Peloponnesus (= "Pelops' island") and was the subject of some special Olympic mythology (see chapter 6).

Besides the animal figurines, an even more impressive group of early dedications are the bronze tripods which have been found at the site. Some of these are immense; the largest is about 10 feet tall. They were of great value in the days before money, and tripods dating from the ninth and eighth centuries have been found in abundance at Olympia. Chariot racing is prominent in Homer, with tripods sometimes the prize. Since he places some chariot races in the district of Elis with a tripod as prize (*Iliad* 11.697), many scholars once thought that these tripods were connected with early races at Olympia, perhaps as prizes which were rededicated by the victors to the god. Recent excavators, however, have discounted this possibility because they accept Pausanias' timetable for the introduction of Olympic events, which places the first chariot races in 680 BC, later than the tripods themselves, and almost a full century after the games began. Yet not everyone is convinced that Pausanias' timetable is completely accurate (see below).

The most recent excavator, Ulrich Sinn, finds the earliest signifi- cance of the site in an oracle of Zeus, consulted especially in matters of war. The geographer Strabo (whose dates span between BC and AD) makes especial note of the oracle, and one of Pindar's poems places the birth of a seer named Iamos at Olympia. Sinn argues that Greeks consulted the Olympic oracle about many battles, including the important battle of Plataea in 479 BC, where a seer from Olympia played an important role.

Olympia enjoys the very oldest Greek temple. The structure known as the Temple of Hera was built here about 600 BC. It is not certain that the temple was always called the Temple of Hera. It may at first have been the temple of Zeus (or Zeus and Hera). Hera would then have inherited it for herself when the new and grander temple of Zeus was built in the 470s (see chapter 5). At any rate, that first temple and some of the "Treasuries" (Pausanias' term), the buildings constructed by individual city-states along the approach to the stadium, were the first structures on the site.

The functions of these treasuries are not fully known. They were indeed used for storage, and perhaps served as a kind of embassy for visitors from the states who built them. The majority of those treasuries belonged to city-states in Magna Graecia, that is, the Greek colonies of Sicily and southern Italy. Those colonies would play an important role in early Olympic athletic history, as well. Olympia was a Panhellenic site, and attracted people from everywhere in the Greek world. Yet Greeks moved by boat, and Olympia's proximity to Sicily and Italy was significant to its development and history. And conspicuous among the dedications there were the spoils which the western Greek colonists took from peoples whom they conquered in those western regions.

The Evidence

Archaeology tends to confirm, *approximately*, the Olympic starting date at or soon after that which Greeks gave; namely, our 776 BC. That date is several decades before the Greek alphabet and Homer's *Iliad* (see chapter 1). Olympics then took place every four years for more than a millennium, well into the latter days of the Roman

Figure 2.1 Ruins of the temple of Hera, oldest in Greece; photo by author

Empire, as antiquity gave way to the early Middle Ages. Very recent excavations prove that international competition took place later than was thought, to about 400 AD.

We learn much from the archaeologists, but not everything. Several other kinds of sources provide substantial evidence. Closely related to archaeology is the evidence from art, which takes us beyond Olympia into the larger world of ancient athletics. Our knowledge of how the events were actually performed relies heavily on the many pictures of athletes in the paintings which decorate vases unearthed around the Greek world. Fortunately, the most heavily represented period of athletic art is in the Archaic and Classical periods, which interest us most. Experts can usually date those vases within a decade, and often identify the individual painter by name. The scenes which they depict can be subject to differing interpretations, but sometimes are decisive in clarifying ancient technique.

Valuable information comes from the excavated items which have inscriptions on them. Most are written on stones, but occasionally on other media. Some of these go back to Archaic times, and tell us otherwise unknown details about specific athletes or sanctuary rules. Like the vase paintings, these inscriptions give us a direct glimpse into antiquity, without the intervention of time. Yet time often intervenes, anyway; for many inscriptions, again like the vases, are so broken or worn that they tell only part of their story. And the story relates to only one place and one time, the day on which someone finished painting a pot or writing, for example, an epitaph of an athlete.

Traditional literary evidence also takes us beyond Olympia into the whole Greek world and the vast span of time in which athletics took place in it. In antiquity, the Olympics were known for their conservatism, for their regularity and comparative lack of change. But inevitably, any institution with a history more than a thousand years long would experience significant changes over the centuries. Sweeping general statements about the ancient games are difficult, even dangerous to make. What is true at one time is not at another. The evidence does not come from a single stratum.

The long period of time is only one of many difficulties in reconstructing the history of the games. There is simply no evidence known for many things which one wants to learn. Several basic items still remain unclear, such as the length of the ancient distance race, and how victory was determined in the all-around athletic event, the pentathlon. Greeks are not silent about Olympia's history, but the bulk of our literary information on the pre-Roman period, which perhaps interests us most, comes from authors who wrote many centuries after the events they report. Much of what they say is unreliable and sometimes surely false (Glass 2002: 155–6). The farther an author is chronologically from what he reports, the less reliable his information becomes. Few of us would be so gullible as to believe everything published on the Internet. Unfortunately, although many ancient texts are equally unreliable, too many modern authors readily believe almost anything written in antiquity, no matter how late or unlikely. As a result, most studies of the Olympics, both technical and for the public, contain many generalizations which are anachronistic or just plain wrong (Golden 1998: 48–52).

Athletics were an integral part of Greek society. Therefore one finds pertinent information scattered throughout the ancient authors, such as Plato, Sophocles, Demosthenes, and Plutarch. It may occur in texts of any genre, historians, medical writers, ancient commentaries on the ancient poets, philosophers or Latin poets of the Roman Empire. Even early Christian fathers may make a comment relative to Olympics or athletics. Some of these texts are of great importance and useful. The *Epinician Odes* of Pindar, written to celebrate specific victories of individual athletes, well express the athletic spirit and values of the early fifth century BC (see chapter 6). These poems sometimes contain important technical details, as well.

The only treatise on athletics to survive is Philostratus' *Gymnastica*, a third century AD document which focuses on the author's own time, long after the golden age of Greek athletics. Often it is polemical and seems written by someone who has little experience with the subject (Harris 1967: 26). Occasionally, the author seeks to tell something about Olympic beginnings or the earliest Olympiads. Although he clearly has no access to legitimate sources of the early history, and much of what he says seems virtually impossible, many modern critics tend to take him seriously (Gardiner 1930: 155; Drees 1968: 44–5, 66; Scanlon 2002: 35–6, 252–3). Yet some wisely do not (Anderson 1986: 268–81; Golden 1998: 19). Despite its promising title, Philostratus' essay is definitely a disappointment.

A far more helpful text is the guidebook of Pausanias, who visited Olympia in the second century AD. He wrote a detailed account of what he saw and was told. Often, what he was told is of highly doubtful historical accuracy, and his own words may contain a bit of a disclaimer. Pausanias' eyewitness reports and his copies of inscriptions that no longer survive are invaluable. And he may well have used some material that goes back to Hippias of Elis.

Hippias was a fifth century BC local historian from Elis who undertook a history of the Olympics, including a catalogue of the victors. Olympic scholars have determined that any later catalogues for the early years must go back to his list. For each Olympiad in his register, he apparently listed each victor for each event that he knew. Of this work nothing survives but a papyrus fragment, which records the victors for a few important decades in the early fifth century. Its general accuracy is confirmed by information in Pindar's *Odes*. Aristotle reworked Hippias' list, but the text and details are unknown. In the third century AD Julius Africanus produced a list which went down to 217 AD; for the early years he no doubt based it on Hippias or Aristotle. Africanus' work is not extant. In the following century, however, the Christian historian Eusebius copied Africanus' text in a work designed to correlate the various chronologies of the ancient world. This work is preserved, but it lists only the victors in the 200 meters, with occasional comments on other athletes and items.

Pausanias says that the program of events at Olympia developed gradually, and gives a timetable, which may or may not go back to Hippias. Whatever the case, many modern students of the games think that it is accurate. Pausanias claims that in the beginning and for about a half-century, the only event at the Olympic festival was the race of one length of the stadium, the *stade*. At the fourteenth Olympiad, he writes, the sponsors added the two *stade* race called the *diaulos*; and at the next, the distance race. Other events were added on piecemeal, according to the table below.

OLYMPIAD	YEAR	EVENT (AND CLOSEST MODERN EQUIVALENT)
1	776	*Stade* (200 meters)
14	724	*Diaulos* (400 meters)
15	720	*Dolichos* (2,400 meters?)
18	708	Wrestling and pentathlon
23	688	Boxing
25	680	*Tethrippon*, four-horse chariot race

33	648	*Pancration* (no holds barred) and *keles* (horse race)
37	632	*Stade* and wrestling for boys
38	628	Pentathlon for boys (never held again)
41	616	Boxing for boys
65	520	Race in armor (*diaulos* in length)
70	500	Mule-cart race
71	496	*Kalpe*, special type of race for mares
84	444	Mule-cart and *kalpe* races abandoned
93	408	*Synoris*, two-horse chariot race
96	396	Contests for heralds and trumpeters
99	384	Chariot race for teams of four colts
128	268	Chariot race for teams of two colts
131	256	Race for colts
145	200	*Pancration* for boys

The first Olympic victor, all ancient sources agree, was Koroibos of Elis, whose occupation is given as "cook." For almost half a century, the victors generally came from the areas near Olympia, mostly Elis, nearby in the north, and Messene, a city not far to the south. Then athletes from several other places in the Peloponnesus, especially Sparta, took away victories. But even in these earliest years a few victors came from Corinth and Athens, and from as far away as Sicily and Asia Minor. The first chariot victor in 680 BC was Pagondas of Thebes. Many of the rather few seventh century victors who are known continued to be Spartans. But in the early sixth century BC, athletes began to come from all over the Greek world. And a long, impressive series of victories by athletes from Magna Graecia began (see chapter 9).

For many years the Olympics held center stage – indeed, the only regularly recurrent show in Greece. There were other athletic contests. Funeral games still took place now and then (Roller 1981: 1–18). And there probably were competitions at local, annual festivals. But there were no other Panhellenic athletic festivals which drew contestants at a pre-arranged time from all parts of the Greek world. Then after almost two centuries, the institution of the athletic festival itself, fueled by Olympia's increasing success, enjoyed sudden and widespread popularity. There arose a flurry of new recurring

Figure 2.2 The "Big Four" or Circuit

meetings which permanently changed the whole phenomenon of athletic competition.

Within a few short decades, three other major crown festivals were founded. They were the Pythian Games at Delphi, founded in 582 BC, the Isthmian Games at Corinth, in the same year, and the Nemean Games at Nemea, in 573. These three festivals, along with the Olympic Games, made up an athletic "Crown Circuit," or Big Four. Any athlete who was victorious in all four games of the

Circuit was recognized as and given the title *periodonikes* or "Winner of the Circuit."

The Panathenaic Games at Athens, instituted in 566 BC, were not part of this major Circuit. Yet they were clearly recognized as the fifth most important recurrent athletic festival in all of Greece. No doubt a number of lesser games were established in this same brief period; for scores of them existed in less than another century. Greece had begun what is known as its golden age of athletics, which lasted about two centuries. But there is no clearly marked end to the golden age. The term is mainly a convention of outdated Classical scholarship. Many would now extend it much farther, or even to the whole history of the ancient Olympic Games, which outlived all their descendants at these other sites.

3

Athletic Events

At staid Olympia, there were never any musical contests. Some of the other festivals included, even featured, competitions in music. Tradition held that the Pythian Games at Delphi were originally limited to musical events, dating to a time before the athletic events were introduced in 582. No source reports the full musical program there, but one of Pindar's *Pythian Odes* honors a victorious flautist. A list of the Panathenaic musical events (Athens) contains, among others, contests in the lyre (*kithara*), flute, and lyre playing with singing. The last was extremely popular and we may compare these singing lyre players to modern rock musicians. The victor in that event won an unusually valuable prize, greater than the prize in any athletic event and worth almost as much as in the prestigious chariot race (see chapter 8).

Some festivals recognized three age groups: boys, youths, and men. At Olympia, there were only two divisions: men and boys. There is no clear evidence as to the exact ages where these distinctions were drawn. Some of these other festivals had a few athletic events not included at Olympia. But all the events of the Olympics were held at all the other games. The athletic programs at these other sites must have, in the main, followed Olympia as their prototype, so there was a high degree of regularity throughout the festival circuit.

Running Events

"Victory by speed of foot is honored above all." Those are the words of Xenophanes, a sixth century BC philosopher who objected to athletes and their popularity (see chapter 7). The phrase "speed of foot" may recall the words expressed in Homer's *Odyssey* stressing the glory which an athlete may win "with his hands *or with his feet*." The shortest foot race, the *stade*, was one length of the stadium track, the practical equivalent of our 200 meter dash (actually only 192.27 meters at Olympia). Greek tradition held that this 200 meter race was the first and only event held at the first Olympiad in 776 BC.

The name of the winner of the 200 appears first in all lists of victors in any Olympiad. Some people think that the *stade* winner had the year named after him. That is not really true. Most Greek states had other means of dating any given year, usually by the name of one or more political leaders. But when Hippias of Elis compiled his catalogue of victors, the *stade* victor obviously headed his list for each individual Olympiad. Perhaps because the Olympic festival was one of the few truly international institutions in Greece, later Greeks found it convenient to use the sequence of Olympiads as a chronological reference. Thus an entry in Julius Africanus' text will read, for example, "Olympiad 77, Dandis of Argos (won) the stade." Subsequent years within an Olympiad are simply viewed as Olympiad 77, years two, three, and four.

As one would expect, methods of running seem to be no different then from now. Several vase paintings show a group of runners rather close to one another, their bodies pitched forward, their arms making large swings up and down. These are clearly runners in the 200, for modern sprinters look much the same. So also distance runners can be easily identified. Like their modern counterparts, they run upright, with less arc in their leg movements, and their arms dangle comfortably at their sides (figure 3.1). Some of these ancient athletes developed the effective strategy of hanging back with the rest of the pack, reserving some strength until near the end. Then they would suddenly break away from the rest and close with a strong spurt of speed, as if barely tired, passing the

Figure 3.1 Distance runners, British Museum, B.609, b–f Panathenaic vase with distance runners

leaders who became weak and faded. Ancient sources never specify the exact number of laps in the distance race, and modern opinions vary greatly. The most widely accepted number is 20 laps, a distance of a little over 3,845 meters (2.36 miles), more than double our classic distance race of 1,500 meters.

The ancient stadium was shaped very differently from the modern one. It was almost twice as long as ours, and about half as wide (figure 3.2). There was no course around an infield, no infield at all, just adjacent lanes for the runners. The athletes had therefore

Figure 3.2 The stadium at Olympia today; photo by author

no gradual turns around a curve at each end, as in a modern stadium. Stephen Miller, excavator of Nemea, found a posthole not far from the north end of the stadium. He conjectures that it held a turning post or *kampter*. It is highly likely that, in the distance race, such a single turning post for all athletes was probably used. But in the 400, or *diaulos*, down and back, the runner would need to turn sharply around any *kampter*. Most scholars think that each 400 runner would have had his own individual turning post. Otherwise there would have been too much congestion at that only turn.

The running style in the 400 would have been closer to that of a sprint than a distance race, but we have no certain depiction of a *diaulos* in progress. A few vases show athletes not patently sprinters or distance runners going around a turning post. In one, a judge stands watch. But if each 400 meter runner had his own turning post, the scene probably shows a distance race. A painting of an athlete about to start, however, certainly shows a *diaulos* runner. In the words written on the vase he is saying in Greek "I am a *diaulos* runner" (Gardiner 1930: figure 90).

At some festivals, such as those at the Isthmos and at the island of Cos, there was a race at a fourth distance, approximately 800 meters, four lengths of the stadium (Bacchylides 10.25). This contest, not on the Olympic program, was called the *hippios*, or "horsey." Because it is neither a sprint nor a distance race, many modern runners think the 800 especially difficult, and might agree that it is more fit for a horse than a human. At Olympia there was only one more running event, the last one ever added to the program, introduced in 520 BC. In this *hoplites* or "armed race" the athletes wore a helmet and carried a shield as they ran the distance of the *diaulos*, the 400. In earlier years they also wore protective greaves on their legs, but that practice was abandoned in the mid-fifth century. The armed runners still ran otherwise nude, like the rest of the athletes (see chapter 9). They carried no weapons.

In modern athletics the shortest sprint is 100 meters, and in indoor contests, even a mere 60. Victory in these races depends strongly on a good start. Even in the modern 200, a bad start will eliminate even the fastest runner. Surely the same was true in antiquity. There has been much controversy about how the ancient foot races began, what starting signals were given, and the nature of any special starting apparatus there might have been. Only one thing is wholly certain: the runners used a standing start, not the start from all fours which is now standard in the shorter modern races.

There are many artistic representations of an individual runner at the start. Vase paintings and plastic art show athletes in two different upright starting positions. In the first of these, the athletes place one foot a few inches in front of the other, the arms stretched forward. In the second starting style, the athletes have their feet and legs together, parallel, and their knees are slightly bent.

At the existing Olympic stadium and many others there remain in the ground stone sills, cut with horizontal grooves. Usually there are two grooves separated by several inches, at what is obviously the starting line. Most historians, encouraged by the stance that shows one foot just before the other, have thought that the barefoot athletes merely set a foot in each of these grooves, and pushed off at the start, gaining a toe-hold by overlapping the front of the groove. Yet that procedure seems rather crude if not dangerous to the feet. And there is a chronological difficulty. None of these stone sills with two grooves is earlier than the Hellenistic age. Yet the vase paintings reveal a surprising and decisive change about 480 BC. All depictions of athletes at the start on vases made before that approximate date exhibit the style with the legs slightly apart. All the runners on vases that date after 480 have the starting position with the legs parallel. There must have been a real change in the starting method, and the chronology argues against the usual notion that the sills alone served the actual start. Perhaps the grooves are all the remains from a more complex starting mechanism.

Until very recently there was no known scene of a group of athletes lined up at the start, something which would let us envision the beginning of an actual race, with all the runners at their marks. In 1989 an Athens art exhibit included a vase which depicts three armed runners apparently along the starting line. The vase, excavated not long before, was virtually unknown, and shows a scene unique to our knowledge. Not only does it reveal three armed runners lined up at the start, but it also seems to illustrate an item that has always before eluded all understanding.

Many literary sources mention an apparatus called a *hysplex* which was used for the start of the foot races. Sometimes it seems to specify a cord strung along in front of the runners; when the cord dropped it was the start of the race. By such means no athlete was able to get a head start. The stance with feet together and knees bent, with a forward lean, suits that interpretation of the *hysplex* well enough. And archaeological remains in the stadium at Cos and elsewhere suggest that they might have served some rather elaborate mechanism. How any such mechanism might work had previously defied all convincing explanation.

The new vase painting of the armed runners almost certainly shows a *hysplex* in position. Indeed, two cords stretch before the athletes; at either end, there seems to be a post. Miller has carefully sought to reconstruct a *hysplex* at the starting sill at Nemea, and he seems to have succeeded. The two posts stand upright, held only by mechanical tension. When they are released they fly forward and down, quickly dropping down the two cords which are stretched between them, one a little higher than the other. The runners, then, up to that point restrained by the *hysplex* cords, are suddenly allowed to speed off. Miller's team finds the result in accord with all the evidence, and I believe his reconstruction is – in the main – correct (Valavanis 1999: 143–72, figure 19). I still see some difficulties. The sills still look rough for barefoot sprinters, and the late chronology of the two grooves remains a problem. In Miller's experiment his runners must be very careful not to trip on the cords lying on the ground in front of them. But nothing in Miller's solution precludes a more complex mechanism that would avoid those difficulties. There may have been more to the *hysplex* apparatus than meets the archaeologists' eyes.

Greek Record Keeping

Their lack of stopwatches obviously prevented the Greeks from giving absolute values to runners' times. But even in events where measurement was easy, such as the discus throw, the marks were not kept for future reference. So Greeks kept no records like our official track and field record marks, measured in minutes and meters. But there are other kinds of records, as in our baseball, tennis, or golf. Many of the items recorded in the *Guinness Book of World Records* are of the same type.

Such records are founded, in simple terms, on who was the first to do the most; the first to win, for example, the British, French, and US Open Championships all twice in a row. The Greeks indeed kept and coveted such records, employing a highly developed system that recorded which athlete was the first to win each event; or who was the first to win a particular combination or number of victories (Young 1997). Various inscriptions express records in such categories as national, family, Olympic, and world records. The formula includes such phrases as "the first ever," "he alone," and my favorite, "no other earthling."

One important category kept track of unprecedented feats in the running events. The first known runner with multiple victories is Pantakles of Athens, who won the Olympic 200 meters in both 696 and 692 BC. In 692 he may have won the 400 meters as well. Chionis of Sparta soon thereafter surpassed Pantakles: he won both 200 meters and 400 meters three Olympiads in a row, 664–656. That record stood for most of two centuries. Yet in 512 BC Phanas of Pellene managed to set a new Olympic running record without needing four Olympiads to surpass Chionis' impressive consistency for three Olympiads. In 520 the armed race was added to the program, enabling Phanas to win three races, 200 meters, 400 meters and armed race at one Olympiad. Africanus lists this feat as a record: the first athlete ever to achieve that triple victory.

In 480 BC Astylos, who formerly competed for Croton, Italy, but that time represented Syracuse, Sicily, won the 200 meters for the third time, and obtained his third 400 crown. He had thus equaled Chionis' record. But he also won the armed race, and thus tied Phanas' record as well. By combining Phanas' versatility with Chionis' multiple victories, he accomplished a unique feat and set a new record. No one had ever won such a combination before.

Contrary to some modern suspicions, neither an athlete nor his fans could misrepresent or exaggerate his exact victories. The whole Greek world was watching and knew the score. A fifth century inscription suggests that Chionis' Spartan countrymen jealously tried to preserve his reputation and his seventh century record. When Astylos set the new Olympic running record, the Spartans carefully added to his memorial stele in Olympia the defensive comment, "There was no armed race in Chionis' time" (Pausanias 6.13.2). Thus they clearly implied that their compatriot Chionis should, to be fair, keep his running record; or had there been an armed race in Chionis' day, the Spartan would have won it, too. At any rate, the Spartans' defensive comment on Chionis' stele testifies to the rigor with which ancient athletic records were kept, and to their international acceptance.

Astylos' record, not surprisingly, stood for more than three centuries. What other runner could be so versatile, and yet maintain an even longer career at the very top? Finally – amazingly – he appeared. Leonidas, an athlete from the island of Rhodes, topped all other records by winning those three races for four Olympiads in a row, 164–152. BC One wishes to know this man's fitness program. Leonidas' record was never tied nor beaten. Perhaps no one even tried. It seems nearly impossible for anyone to stay at peak form for five Olympiads, to run at least thirteen races and never lose. Victory in a sprint is always fragile: one poor start, one bump, one day of a minor illness – or just a "bad day" – could nullify almost two decades of training and planning.

In the Roman Empire excellent runners probably had no hope at all of winning those thirteen races and setting a new Olympic record. In the course of eight centuries, everything had already been done. A dauntless Polites of Caria chose a path perhaps even more difficult than the obvious, but at least it was not a commitment of many years' work and self-sacrifice. It could, in fact, be done in one day – if the world's best sprinter could become the world's best distance runner.

Everything, after all, had not been done, because everyone for eight centuries had assumed that a sprint and distance combination was impossible. But Polites trained for it and did it, setting the new running record with which this book began. I am rather certain that he would not have trained for both the 200 meters and the distance race had there not been that background of eight centuries and had the Greeks kept records based on absolute marks in minutes. But Polites' achievement, in Pausanias' words this "great marvel" (6.13.3), remains as a monument to the longevity of the ancient Olympics and to the Greeks' "pursuit of individual excellence."

The Pentathlon

The modern pentathlon is a military-oriented event created in 1912. It has nothing in common with the ancient pentathlon. The modern "all-around" contest is the decathlon, a grueling combination of four running events and six field events, which take place over two days. The Olympic victor wins the unofficial but well-recognized title, "World's Best Athlete." The ancient all-around event, the *pentathlon,* was completed in a single day. It combined the three ancient field events – discus, long jump, and javelin – with one running event – the 200 meters – and a wrestling contest at the end. Some ancient authors say there was a time when each of the three field events was contested separately, a winner named for each (Pindar *Isthmian* 1.26; Philostratus *Gym.* 3). In Homer, all competitions are separate, with nothing like a pentathlon.

By its very nature, the combination of the five different events necessarily originated as an invention of some specific people at some specific time and place. But there is no reliable report of that occasion, nor any historical athletic festival when the five were not combined. Even more frustrating are the scanty – but confused – hints in ancient sources about the method which determined victory in the pentathlon. Each of the many modern theories about how the victor was determined is impossible unless one or more of these hints is simply rejected as false (more likely than a change of method over the years). In the rather rare case that any one athlete won all the first three events, he was declared winner and the contest was finished. But beyond that rare case, all else is conjecture. Sources do indicate, however, that often the overall contest was not decided until it ended in a wrestling final.

There is no direct evidence for the theory that is most popular among scholars. This theory maintains that every pentathlete was in individual competition with each of the others (something like "side-pots" in poker). Anyone who was defeated three times by another contestant was eliminated, no matter what finishing position either one had occupied in the first three or four events. This system still leaves the (unlikely) mathematical possibility that as many as six athletes remained in contention before the fifth event, wrestling. Such an unusual case would require a quarter-final and two byes. But ordinarily there would be no more than four athletes left, so that semi-finals in the wrestling would narrow the contestants to two for the decisive last bout. Yet I stress that available evidence will *not* definitively explain how first place in the pentathlon was determined.

A boys' division of the pentathlon was introduced in the early days of the Olympic Games, but was abandoned right away. There was a boys' pentathlon at Delphi and elsewhere, but not at Nemea. The 200 meter event in the pentathlon would have been exactly like the open race except run separately from it. The rules and manner of the wrestling contest would not have differed from the separate wrestling event (see chapter 4).

Discus

No event typifies ancient athletics so much as the discus throw, a uniquely Greek concept never practiced by others (except the modern Greeks: see chapter 13) until the first Olympiad sponsored by the International Olympic Committee in Athens, 1896 (hereafter, the IOC). In art, Greeks at the gym may carry a discus around in a sack, somewhat as one of us might carry gym shoes in a bag; and discuses often hang from a wall in the background of gymnasium scenes. Contests in throwing a rock for distance are natural enough,

and in nineteenth-century England "throwing the stone" was a regular athletic event, precursor to the modern shot put. Boys everywhere
have probably always made flat rocks skip on a body of water.
Today, there are lightweight disks called frisbees which sail through
the air, and even competitions in that activity. But the ancient
discus throw, like its modern descendant, entailed the rotation of a
heavy flat disk intended to sail through the air like a frisbee.

The discuses excavated, as well as those represented in art, vary
greatly in size and material. They are of stone or metal, the latter
usually in cast bronze, and most of them weigh between 2 and 4
kilos. The variety of size and weight results in part from the amount
of wear, but also because the official size differed from place to
place. And there were discuses for children. But the average weight
tends to be a little more than 2 kilos, and the modern standard of
2 kilos (4 lb. 6.4 oz.) is based on a few of those excavated at Olympia.

The main question about the nature of the ancient throw concerns whether or not the athletes executed a full rotation of the
body. One theory has ancient athletes spinning to use their own
centrifugal force, much like the current method. Another theory
maintains that they threw using arm strength alone, perhaps with
some body twist, but not a full spin as in our event. The weight of
opinion, including most recent opinion, is strongly against the spin.
But in view of the artistic evidence, as well as that in literature,
I strongly favor the theory of the full spin.[1] A number of discus
throwers on the vases have their weight distributed on their feet in
a position much like that of modern athletes, and they might even
lose their balance without the force of the body rotation.

Long Jump

How the ancient long jump was performed is the most complex
question of method in the study of any ancient event; and it has
created more controversy in modern interpretations then any other.
A large part of the confusion results from reports which state that
two early ancient athletes, Phayllos of Croton and Chionis of Sparta,
jumped beyond 50 feet. Almost all modern theories seek to account
for so long a distance. Both reports are clearly false, appearing in

questionable texts dating from more than half a millennium after the supposed jumps.

Too many scholars tend to accept anything stated in antiquity, no matter how unreliable its source (see chapter 2). In the nineteenth century someone even theorized that the Greeks used a springboard to achieve such distances. The most popular theories involve multiple jumps which when added together would total more than 50 feet. For a long time the triple jump theory prevailed, partly because in the early years of modern track and field, 50 feet was a good triple jump. For the last several decades, however, many scholars have accepted the hypothesis of the eminent German scholar, Joachim Ebert (1963: 2–34); namely, that the ancient jump consisted of a series of five standing jumps. But the evidence from art clearly excludes any possibility of a standing jump.

All ancient art, and even the literary evidence, is consonant with a single running jump, much the same as ours. Gardiner (1910: 310; 1930: 152–3) saw the truth long ago, and simply rejected the two reports of 50-foot jumps as bogus. The real difficulty is explaining how the jumpers used the weights, called *halteres* or "jumpers." The *halteres*, one held in each hand, appear on every picture of ancient long jumping. A number of these weights of varying size and shape have been excavated. Greek authors say that their purpose is to help the jumper go further (Aristotle, *Progression of Animals* 705a; cf. Philostratus *Gym.* 55). One naturally wonders how extra weight can make an athlete jump farther. In modern experiments, the weights have slowed jumpers down, and shorter distances result, not longer. But modern experiments have lasted only a few hours, and ancient athletes had centuries to develop the right technique. A jumper in the nineteenth century who was trained in the use of weights reportedly leaped 29 feet 7 inches using them, just beyond the current (2003) world record of 29 feet 4 inches, set by Mike Powell in Tokyo, 1991 (Gardiner 1930: 151).

The element which modern studies have not taken into account is height. The higher a long jumper goes, the farther he goes, simply because he does not come down so soon. Speed and height are the main, if not the only factors in long jumping. If swung upwards at just the right time, it seems certain that the weights would lift an athlete higher than his normal jump. Although the

Figure 3.3 Long jumper at take-off; Boston Museum of Fine Arts, 10.176, r–f skyphos, by the Brygos Painter

added weight would slow the jumper down in his approach, apparently the added height compensated for that loss of speed, and the net result was better with the weights. The athletes also threw the weights backwards as they landed, thus gaining a little push at the end.

The precise timing of swinging the weights in the approach and take-off would have been crucial. And in the need for careful timing we can find the best explanation as to why a flautist regularly accompanies a long jumper in ancient paintings. The ancient jump, then, was almost certainly a single running jump, performed by athletes well trained in a precision feat. Ancient jumpers did not attain 50 feet, but surely, with this mechanical help, they would have achieved excellent marks by our standards (see appendix B).

Javelin

One cannot hope that the archaeologist's spade will turn up an ancient javelin, since they were made of wood. Pictures show an implement clearly lighter than ours, and slightly shorter. As in the long jump, the Greeks used mechanical assistance. The athlete wrapped a thin leather thong more than a foot long tightly around the javelin near its middle, and made a loop at the end of it. He then inserted two fingers through the loop to keep the loop taut as he held the javelin in his hand, and kept that grip throughout the approach run and start of the throw, until the moment of release.

The use of such a thong, in Greek called an *ankyle* and in Latin *amentum*, was not a peculiarity of athletics. The Greeks fitted the military javelin with a similar device, as did many other peoples of Europe, both in antiquity and much later. Its purpose was twofold: it extended the point of release several inches beyond the natural length of the thrower's arm. More importantly, the unwinding of the thong rotated the javelin so strongly that there was a rifling effect, which made the javelin fly farther and truer.

Military scenes on the vases often show a javelin with a metal point, but in athletic scenes no metal tip or other special point is visible at the end of the object. At Nemea, Miller has indeed found some metal points for javelins. It is not certain, however, that these come from an athletic context. In light of the artistic evidence, I suspect that these, too, were probably for military use, perhaps even from dedications.

The effectiveness of the *amentum* cannot be doubted. Ancient Greeks and others assumed that it was a great help. And experiments from Napoleon's time to ours prove that the device increases accuracy and landing on point. The distances achieved are greatly increased, according to some reports even doubled, which seems rather unlikely. But that distance was improved somewhere between 15 percent and 35 percent seems highly likely.

Frequent modern comments that the javelin was dangerous to the spectators, occasionally killing an onlooker, are groundless. There is no historical record of such an accident in competition. Rather, these ideas result from fictitious items. First, Antiphon, a fifth century BC Athenian orator, politician, and speech professor, prepared an assignment for prospective legal advocates. In it he asks his students to practice their skills by defending an athlete against an imaginary murder charge (*Tetralogia* 2.4). The charge results from a hypothetical fatal accident which occurred when the accused was throwing his javelin in a gymnasium. Second, there has been confusion with some myths, such as that in which Apollo unwittingly kills his young lover Hyacinthus with an errant discus throw (not a javelin).

4

Combat and
Equestrian Events

Wrestling

Wrestling metaphors permeate Greek literature. They are frequent in all three tragedians, the comic playwright Aristophanes, the orators, and philosophers (Herrmann 1995: 77–84). Authors knew they could count on their audience's knowledge of the techniques employed in wrestling, because it was the one athletic activity practiced by almost all freeborn men in Greek society. Greeks would often go to their nearest "wrestling club" building (*palaestra*) for a workout and social chatting. The *palaestra* was usually a rather large, square building with rooms to serve the athletes in various ways built around an open central courtyard, the wrestling area proper. Other combative sports took place there, as well. We may compare our golf or tennis club. Some of the wrestling buildings were public property, associated with a public gym, but others were separate, privately owned institutions. Many *palaestrae* focused on the physical training of boys, but older youths and men used them as well. Information on admission, membership, tuition, and other regulations is scanty and diverse.

Our so-called "Greco-Roman" wrestling is a modern creation, with little, if any, relationship to ancient Greece. There is no point in seeking the origin of wrestling with rules, which one ancient scholar even attributed to Theseus of Greek mythology. The only style of wrestling contested at Olympia was the classic Greek upright wrestling called *pale*.[1] There was seldom any brutality. Greek wrestling was a contest of strength, balance, and especially technical know-how. The object was to throw one's opponent so that his back, shoulder, or hip touched the sandy surface on which they stood. One scene shows an umpire looking carefully to make his judgment.

Like a tennis match of sets, victory went to the first man to achieve three falls. On vases and coins we see the throws known to modern wrestling events: the "flying mare," various neck and body holds, and body throws. One scene shows an athlete who has tried to trip his opponent, but he himself is being tossed backwards because the opponent grasped the tripping leg and thrust it up and back. All these throws and moves were carefully practiced and planned. There survives a small portion of a second century AD manual for coaches to use in practice drills. There are two students, here called A and B (Pap. Oxy. 3.466; Poliakoff 1987: 51–3):

> You (A) Stand beside him and grab his head inside your right arm. You (B) Throw your arms around him. You (A) Get out from under him. You (B) Step in and mix it up. You (A) Get under with your right. You (B) Counter that and take him from the side with your left. You (A) Shove him back with *your* left.

Regrettably, the papyrus is fragmented in the middle, and it is not easy to make good sense of the Greek, anyway. The most famous and marvelous Greek athlete of all, Milo of Croton, was a wrestler. After his death he became the subject of many tales, some real and confirmed by reliable sources, others no doubt imaginary (see chapter 9).

Boxing

Boxing is represented in Greece from the Mycenaean period and the Greek dark ages, long before the Olympic Games began. Yet the earliest depiction of formal athletics in the Mediterranean world is far earlier. It comes from the island of Santorini (Greek Thera), the island so renowned for its volcanic activity that a few wrongly claim it was the lost Atlantis. The city of Akrotiri in Thera was covered by volcanic ash in about 1600 BC, and offers a window into the past, like Pompeii – only much older. A fresco from Akrotiri shows two young boxers squaring off. They wear a glove on one hand only, while the other is bare. They have simple belts around their waists, no loincloth.

These details have seemed perplexing, but the most likely explanation is that the contest includes both boxing and belt wrestling. Belt wrestling, where one fighter grabs the other's belt for control or a throw, appears in ancient Egypt and several other places even in modern times. There are boxing scenes on some geometric pots, but they are so stylized that the presence or absence of a belt cannot be determined. Boxers in Homer wear a belt with no self-evident purpose; perhaps it is simply a memory of an earlier time. In literature and art of the historic period, boxers are as nude as the rest of the athletes.

The rules of Greek boxing seem odd to us. There were no rounds. The athletes kept fighting until one of them could no longer continue or formally admitted defeat. There were no weight divisions. Boys and men of normal size boxed in their local *palaestrae*. But only men of "heavyweight" size competed at major festivals, such as the Olympics. Even the vases for Panathenaic victors depict only exceptionally big men. There is little or no evidence that body blows were part of a normal bout. All punches appear to be directed at the head. Several vase scenes represent clear knockouts; others, a distressed athlete signaling his capitulation by raising high a finger of one hand.

From the outset of history, in Homer and in the earliest vase paintings, Greek boxers wore coverings on their hands. The earliest forms, *himantes*, were merely strips of rawhide wrapped tightly around the forearm and hand, the fingers left open. Their purpose was probably more to protect the hands of the attacking boxer than to soften the blow. When unwound, these leather thongs were long and cumbersome. A boxer needed to wrap them carefully before any bout or serious practice. In the fourth century BC an easier and softer glove appeared, perhaps used only in practice. At the same time, the "sharp thongs" appeared in competition. These were already wrapped and could be pulled over the hand without rewrapping them each time. Hard leather strips lay over the knuckles, but the fingers were still bare. The sharp thongs covered most of the forearm, and the top end was fitted with a wool band much like the sweatbands we use in tennis. The boxers could have used them to wipe off sweat, but they no doubt needed them to wipe away blood, as well.

The sharp thongs were a precursor to brass knuckles, but boxing was always brutal and bloody. One very early vase painting vividly depicts blood streaming from a boxer's nose (figure 4.1). There are reports of boxers occasionally dying from their injuries. In all the combative events in all four major Greek festivals from the beginning to the end, there is evidence for only six to eight athletes who died in competition (Brophy 1985: 172; Scanlon 2002: 304). That does not seem many in view of all those centuries and the rather frequent deaths in modern boxing, where the conditions are presumed to be safer.

At least half these deaths were in boxing, and all but one or two at Olympia. The prestige of an Olympic victory probably induced the athletes to fight longer and to risk more than in the other games. That may well be the case in the latest of these deaths, which we know only from a terse second century AD inscription now in the museum at Olympia. The epitaph tells the viewer that a man named "Camel," a Nemean victor, died at Olympia in a boxing match: "He prayed to Zeus for the crown or death. 35 years old."

Pancration

In the past decade, in North and South America, at least, an old activity has turned up as a kind of shocking novelty. Some call it a sport, others refuse to dignify it with that name. It is a combative event where virtually anything is allowed: kicking, blows anywhere, head-butts, submission holds, choke holds, and so on. Such unrestricted fighting has always been recognized; in England they call it "all-in" fighting, while Americans tend to call it "no holds barred." It has received only a small degree of institutionalization in the modern world, more likely held in illegal venues than with society's sanction. Promoters can in many places now organize such contests, and they are taped for television.

Figure 4.1   A bloody boxing match; British Museum, b–f Ampbhora, B.295

Most people call these new contests "ultimate fighting," but some even still use the ancient Greek name, *pancration.* The word means "every (form of) power." The presence of such an event as an integral part of the Olympic program surprises those who are overly credulous about the "glories of ancient Greece," and often even idealize ancient Greeks as a people with especial restraint and humanity. The *pancration* was anything but restrained – a free combination of boxing, wrestling, and street fighting which went on, as in boxing, until one contestant could no longer continue or gave a formal sign that he gave up. Sources say that only two acts were forbidden, eye-gouging and biting: both fouls well illustrated on the vases, with judges ready to intervene. Another vivid scene shows a pancratiast on top of his adversary, one hand over the downed athlete's mouth so that he can breathe only through his nose. But the other arm of the athlete with the advantage is cocked ready to come straight down on his opponent's nose. One must assume the bout could not last much longer.

The modern *pancration* revival tends to confirm a suspicion that the ancient contests might end quickly. On some occasions, the bouts are extended, lasting more than several minutes. In these cases one athlete maintains a wrestling hold on his opponent, who cannot extricate himself, but is able to prolong the matter, some-times even until he can reverse the advantage. But other modern matches last only fifteen or twenty seconds before one fighter is so clearly beaten that he concedes. A seasoned professional athlete would usually have capitulated before suffering a serious and per-haps lasting injury. In the *pancration* that point is probably easier to determine than in boxing; the result is fewer deaths (above).

Yet the Olympics are like nothing else, and a pancratiast's desire to win could overcome any concern for safety. The posthumous victory of Arrichion was the most storied athletic death. In the Olympic *pancration* final of 564 BC, the two-time defending Olym-pic champion Arrichion found himself in a lethal choke hold, just as he got a good grip on his adversary's ankle. In a final extra effort, the sources say, just as Arrichion expired, he dislocated his opponent's ankle. The opponent, not knowing Arrichion was dying, lifted his finger to signal his own defeat. The officials did not hesitate to give the victory to Arrichion.

We need not look to Rome to realize that at some periods vio-lence itself may have amazing spectator appeal. In our time, profes-sional (dramatic) wrestling is highly popular, even though the spectators generally know that all the violent action is staged, not real. Much of our own entertainment in movies and television is founded on the principle that violence "sells." Violence actually dominates the new computer games. In the Greek Archaic and Classical periods, the *pancration* was ranked of no more importance than any other event, and still overshadowed by the 200 meter sprint. But after several centuries, the violence of the *pancration* gained more and more attention and prominence. In some local and regional festivals the *pancration* prizes became more valuable than others. For centuries there was no boys' *pancration* at the Olympic or Pythian Games; but it was added to the Pythian Games in 346 BC, and even conservative Olympia introduced the event in 200 BC.

Record Keeping: The Combat Events

One of the most fabled ancient athletes was Theogenes of Thasos. In the 480 BC Olympics, Theogenes entered both the boxing and the no holds barred. In boxing, he dethroned the defending champion Euthymos of Greek Italy (see chapter 9). But exhausted or injured from this boxing final, Theogenes was unable to compete in the *pancration* final, and his scheduled opponent in that event won by forfeit. The Olympic officials, apparently embarrassed by his "no-show," fined Theogenes an amount of money equal to several hundreds of thousands of dollars. He easily paid.

Pausanias says that Theogenes entered both the boxing and the *pancration* because "he wished to win both events at the same time." He sought a record (see chapter 3): "first man ever to win both *pancration* and boxing," and he hoped for a "same day" double. In the next Olympiad the officials barred him from defending his crown in the boxing, but permitted his entry in the *pancration*. This time he won that event. That *pancration* victory, joined to his earlier boxing crown, enabled him to achieve his goal: the first man ever to combine victories in both those Olympic combative events. He thus set a new record, and the first item in his victory inscription announces it: "Never before was the same man crowned at Olympia winning in both boxing and pankration." His Isthmian record was similar, but even better: "In nine Isthmiads, ten victories. For twice the herald proclaimed him "the only man on earth to win both boxing and pancration in a single day" (Dittenberger No. 36; Ebert 1972: 37).

Theogenes was an exceptional athlete, and clearly more versatile than the boxers and pancratists of the Archaic period who had preceded him. Yet an even more versatile athlete was still to come – in about two and a half centuries; namely, Kleitomachos of Thebes. Kleitomachos won the *pancration* in 216 BC, and returned to Olympia in 212 as defending *pancration* champion. In 212 he entered both the *pancration* and the boxing. He was following the path of Theogenes in 480. Another athlete, too, Kapros of Elis, wished to double in 212. But he did not enter the boxing at all; he entered the *pancration* and the wrestling. The wrestling took place first of the three combative events, and Kapros won it.

Kleitomachos had not yet competed when he proposed that the *pancration* contest be moved ahead of the boxing, apparently regarding the boxing as the more likely to produce an injury. He probably remembered Theogenes' fate. The officials agreed. But Kleitomachos then lost his *pancration* crown to Kapros, and Kapros thus achieved his own double victory, wrestling and *pancration*. Kleitomachos went on to win the boxing. That victory, along with the *pancration* crown from the previous Olympiad, made him, as Pausanias (6.15.3–5) duly notes, "The first man since Theogenes," some 277 years before, to win that difficult Olympic double.

Kleitomachos was thus able only to tie, not to break, Theogenes' record. He had tried to break it. That is why he entered the *pancration* again in 212, even though he already had won it in 216. For Theogenes' double came in two parts, two separate Olympiads. Had Kleitomachos won both events on that one day in 212, he would have broken the record, which would then have read: "Kleitomachos was the first man on earth to win both boxing and *pancration* at Olympia on the same day." But the new record fell that particular day not to Kleitomachos, but to his pancratiast foe, the double victor Kapros. Pausanias (6.15.10) carefully phrases Kapros' new record and a new title that entered the official record: "Kapros was the first man since Herakles" to win both *pancration* and wrestling. Herakles, of course, is a mythical athletic figure. This title was probably political, designed to match Kleitomachos' title, "First since Theogenes" (who was already assuming some of the legendary qualities of the heroes of Greek myth).

I return to Kleitomachos of Thebes, who lost the 212 BC *pancration* to Kapros and managed to tie (but not break) Theogenes'

Olympic record. He had a far better day at the Isthmian Games soon thereafter. He finally broke one of Theogenes' old records. I translate the inscription from the base of his statue at Thebes (Ebert 1972: 67):

> Just as you see, friend, the bronze strength of this statue of Kleitomachos, so Greece saw the might of the man. No sooner did he undo from his hands the bloody *boxing* gloves but he was doing battle in the fierce pancration. In the *third* event, he did not sand his shoulders; but *wrestled* without being thrown, to take his third first prize from the Isthmus. He is the *only* man of Greece to achieve this feat.

Theogenes' Isthmian record was especially difficult to surpass. Not only did he win the boxing and *pancration* there "on the same day," but he also did it twice. Studying Theogenes' Isthmian record, Kleitomachos would immediately see that the approach which he used wisely enough, but without success at Olympia, could not succeed at the Isthmia. At the Isthmia, mere victories in boxing and *pancration*, even on the same day, would not even tie the record. Theogenes had already done that twice. Like Polites (see chapter 3), instead of pursuing a risky and arduous long-term extension of his career, he decided to diversify even further. Whatever we may think of the combative events and their participants, any man who became a master of all three, then won them all one right after another at one of the Big Four Crown Games, is extraordinary. We should not begrudge him his unique title.

Equestrian Events

Horse races and chariot races played a featured role in the Olympics and other major ancient athletic festivals. Obviously, Greeks recognized that these events differed in their very nature from the human competitions, but they thought that the two types of contests belonged together. They regarded the four-horse chariot race as the highlight and most prestigious event of the festival meeting. At the Panathenaic Games, for example, the prize was larger than that for any athletic event. Pindar's poems are arranged in an order that places the more important victories first. The *Olympian Odes* precede Pindar's other three "books," and within each book the equestrian poems come ahead of those for the athletes.

In the *Iliad* Agamemnon says that any man who had the prizes which his team of race horses had won would be "rich in gold" (9.123–7). Yet to raise horses for competition was not a money-making occupation for anyone in private enterprise. To keep stables in antiquity was extremely expensive. The cost of keeping a horse for one year was apparently equivalent to the annual pay of five soldiers or the purchase price of several slaves. Horse racing even then was the "sport of kings" and the wealthy. Although ancient Athens is known as the "cradle of democracy," ancient Greece, especially Archaic Greece, still had strong divisions of wealth and social class.

Art regularly depicts the Greek horse as rather small, with thick shoulders, and a smartly erect head. Perhaps such a horse was introduced to Greece by very early invaders. The Greeks adopted the use of horses rather late compared with the ancient cultures of the Near East. Evidence of their use does not begin until about 1600 BC. But they are well known in Mycenaean Greece, where they were highly esteemed and played a role in warfare. Olympia itself was early and strongly associated with horses. Horses are prominent among the many animal figurines, both terracotta and bronze, which excavators have found in early strata there. And in Homer, Elis (later, at least, the administrative seat of Olympia) is explicitly mentioned as a site of chariot races (*Iliad* 11.697) – where the prizes were tripods, another distinctive feature of early Olympia according to the results of archaeology (see chapter 2).

Pausanias' timetable dates the inception of chariot racing at Olympia to 680 BC, almost a full century after the first foot race began it all in 776. All events for athletes were well established by 680. In a place so early and strongly associated with horses, one would hardly expect the first equestrian event to come so late. Yet Pausanias' timetable may not be wholly accurate (see chapter 2).

The four-horse chariot, *tethrippon*, was the first Olympic equestrian event on the program of an Olympiad, although Homer's warriors used a two-horse chariot in the Funeral Games of Patroclus.

Figure 4.2   Tethrippon, four-horse chariot; Boston Museum of Fine Arts, 00330, b–f Panel Amphora, painted by "Group E"

Strangely, Pausanias states that the race for those two-horse chariots (*synoris*) was the very last regular event introduced to the program. His date is 408 BC, more than two centuries after the athletic program was complete. The regular mounted horse race (*keles*) had long been in place, and some other events on the hippodrome had been briefly held and then abandoned (the *apene* and *kalpe*, below).

Scenes on vases represent the chariot used in the *tethrippon* as much like that which Homer described for two horses: a simple, lightweight chariot, not much more than a platform on two wheels. The charioteer stood upright on the platform holding the reins. The two central horses were yoked, but the outer two were "trace-horses," that is, not yoked and used as much for control as power. The tack was rather simple. Pindar presents the invention of the bridle and bit as one of the great discoveries of mankind (*Olympian* 13.63–86). But the Greeks never discovered a harness that would use a collar to place the pull and strain mainly on the shoulders of the horse. Instead, a strap went horizontally across the front of the horse's throat, and must have had a tendency to cut off its air and choke it.

The chariot used in the *synoris*, the race for two yoked horses, was usually similar to that of the *tethrippon*. Some paintings, however, at least for the games at Athens, show it as a cart in which the driver sits in a kind of chair. A similar cart was used in a rather strange event called the *apene*. It was a race for mule-carts which was introduced into the official Olympic program in 500 BC, but abandoned not long thereafter in 444. Pausanias suggests that the Eleans probably terminated it because they believed they were under an ancient curse if a mule was ever born in their country. And he himself says that the mule-cart was not very ancient or attractive (5.9.2).

The mule and mule-cart attracted a mixed reaction in Greece. Some apparently shared Pausanias' contempt; there is a tale that at first the poet Simonides disdained to write a victory ode for an *apene* victor. But despite Pausanias' remark, mule-carts seem indeed to be very ancient. Priam came to ransom Hector's body in a mule-cart, which Homer describes in almost loving detail (*Iliad* 24.265–74). The colonists of Magna Graecia, in particular, seem to have used and admired mules. Perhaps these western Greeks had prevailed on the Olympic officials to undertake the event. They made up the majority of known mule-cart victors, and even wealthy Sicilian monarchs competed and were victorious in that race. Obviously, some mule-cart victors were very proud of it. Anaxilas, the monarch of Rhegium, commemorated his victory by stamping one of his coins with an *apene*; and two of Pindar's fourteen *Olympic Odes* are for prominent Sicilians who won in the mule-cart race.

Another event rather difficult for us to imagine was equally short-lived at Olympia. The *kalpe* was introduced in 496 and abandoned along with the mule-cart in 444. Here the driver rode in a cart pulled by mares. There is little detailed information about what took place in the *kalpe*. It appears certain that it, too, was for a rider on a cart. But here the driver dismounted at one or more points of the race, and ran alongside his mares holding the reins. He was probably on foot at the finish line. Although abandoned rather soon at the Olympics, a similar race not restricted to mares long continued at the games at Athens and a few other places.

Only the *kalpe* was limited by gender at Olympia. In all other equestrian events mares and stallions were equals. Mares appear as early as Homer and were often successful. Teams of mares won major chariot victories at Olympia, and Pausanias tells the story of a mare named Aura who threw her rider early in the race, but continued anyway, and won. Pausanias states that the officials allowed her owner to retain his victory. No new equestrian events were added after the *synoris* in 408, but a new age category for foals was intermittently incorporated: for the four-horse chariot in 384 BC, the two-horse, in 264, and the regular horse race (*keles*), in 256, all for foals.

The chariot races were long: the four-horse probably about 8.5 miles and the two-horse almost 6 miles. The mounted *keles* event was much shorter, most likely just one circuit of the hippodrome racetrack, perhaps not much more than two-thirds of a mile. Professional jockeys almost always rode the mounts, but the owners of the stable received the victory. Art, with a few unexplained exceptions, depicts the jockeys as very small men, like ours. They held the reins with one hand, and used a goad with the other.

Like the athletes proper, the jockeys competed nude. This extreme version of riding bareback surprises, since Greeks had saddles. The jockeys just did not use them in these races. A much greater handicap was the complete absence of stirrups, which were not invented until much later. The charioteers, like the jockeys, were ordinarily professional drivers. They were the only contestants at the festival to be clothed. They wore long white gowns such as the distinguished looking "Statue of a Charioteer" found and now prominently displayed at Delphi (late Archaic, bronze; Drees 1968: plate 10). As in the horse races, the owners, not the drivers, were declared the victors.

As a few of our own outstanding racehorses, such as Seabiscuit and Secretariat, have themselves become famous, a few individual horses in antiquity had exceptional reputations. The best known and most remarkable was Pherenikos (Bring-Victory), a horse owned by Hieron, the monarch of Syracuse, Sicily. Pherenikos won for Hieron two Olympic and two major Pythian victories from 482 to 472, a very long career for a racehorse.

From the start, the chariot race was a favorite of literary authors as well as the spectators. Before the race in the *Iliad*, Nestor gives his son Antilochus elaborate instructions on managing his chariot, and Homer dwells far longer on the chariot race than all the other events taken together. One of the more prominent passages in Greek tragedy is a long section of Sophocles' *Electra*, in which a disguised Orestes vividly but falsely recounts how he himself, Orestes, was killed in a multiple crash in a chariot race at Delphi.

The crashes were apparently a major attraction of the chariot races; one thinks of the way the danger of collisions in modern auto racing appeals to its fans. A passage in Pindar implies that only one charioteer of forty actually finished a *tethrippon* (four-horse) race at Delphi (*Pythian* 5.49–53).[2] As in auto racing, sometimes an ancient crash was fatal to the driver. A fragment of an Aeschylus play is preserved mainly because of its sensationalistic sketch of a chariot crash: "chariot on top of chariot, corpse on corpse; there were horses piled on horses in great confusion (*frag.* 38 Radt).

There was one more category on the Olympic program; namely, the contests to determine who would become the announcer (*keryx*) and the trumpeter (*salpinktes*) for the festival. These events, both begun in 396 BC, took place before all the others. The trumpeter called the crowd to attention before the *keryx* gave announcements preceding and following each event.[3] The *salpinktes* also apparently signaled the last lap in races at the hippodrome by giving a trumpet blast, just like the "gun lap" in our track events.

Zeus Country

Most details of the very early centuries of the Olympics are wholly unknown, obscure, or clouded in myth. Yet thanks to archaeology and a few good ancient sources, we can determine or reasonably conjecture much of what we wish to know. Even when known, however, the events of these years can seldom be dated precisely. All the earliest dates here are merely approximate.

Sometime in the tenth century BC, the local inhabitants of this fertile valley established a cult of the god Zeus. Soon they built an altar for the sacrifices they made to him. They brought many dedications to the site, mostly animal figurines and the large tripods. Perhaps before the Olympics began, these people also founded a cult for the mythological hero Pelops. But what was later called the tomb of Pelops was apparently a cenotaph, and archaeology cannot prove the antiquity that some, both ancient and modern, had attributed to it. Ulrich Sinn (2000: 15–22), a recent excavator of Olympia, thinks that the oracle of Zeus was the focal point of the entire early cult.

Sometime in the early or mid-eighth century BC, the managers of the sanctuary incorporated one or more athletic contests as part of the veneration of Zeus. The traditional date for the first Olympics, our 776 BC, suits all the literary evidence well, and does not clash significantly with the archaeological remains. Another recent excavator, Mallwitz, argues for a date just a few decades later, relying mainly on his dating of some wells. But to postpone the date of the first Olympics, he must propose that the first several Olympiads were held every year instead of every four years (Mallwitz 2002: 96–101). I think it more reasonable to assume a few decades without wells than to imagine annual Olympics when no literary source suggests them. In the traditional timetable for the introduction of each event, the first thirteen Olympiads, until 724 BC, consisted of nothing but the 200 meter dash. The chariot races, accordingly, were not inaugurated until the games were nearly a century old, 680 BC. There are reasons for some doubt about this scheme; but there is no means of resolving the difficulty, since we have complete records for only the 200 meters, anyway (see chapter 2). There would seem, however, little need for many wells at the outset.

After about 700 BC the expanding program and importance of the festival began to attract so many people that the custodians of the site were indeed compelled to find ways to provide them with water. The festival took place in August, when sometimes it is so blisteringly hot at Olympia that one wonders about the wisdom of having a gathering there at this time. To sate the thirst of the visitors the officials dug numerous wells north of the athletic track, which we could probably call a stadium at this point. Olympia's relationship with the Greeks of Magna Graecia began to increase, bringing more and more dedications. Southwest of the sanctuary itself, a meadow was leveled off and developed as a place where the festival-goers could camp and picnic. Their presence no doubt summoned the food-sellers and others who hawked the items which people hawk at any such assemblage.

One celebrated feature of the Altis, the sanctuary at Olympia, was its "sacred olive tree." In Pindar's *Olympian* 3, Herakles fetches the tree for the Olympic olive from the land of the Hyperboreans, a people who, the Greeks said, lived "north of north." Far from frigid, this mythical land enjoyed an exceptionally mild climate and the people an exceptionally mild way of life. They experienced no sickness, no old age, no war (Pindar, *Pythian* 10.36–44). There is no way to know when and where any specific tree in the sanctuary's grove was identified and designated as the "Sacred Olive." But author after author recognizes its special role at Olympia. From that particular tree the sponsors cut the olive branches that were given as the victor's prize. And the olive branch as a symbol – sometimes

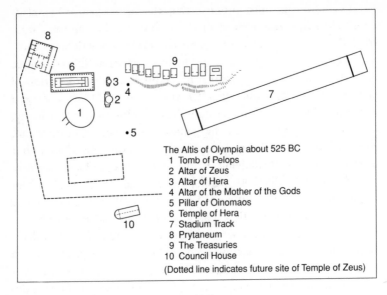

The Altis of Olympia about 525 BC
1 Tomb of Pelops
2 Altar of Zeus
3 Altar of Hera
4 Altar of the Mother of the Gods
5 Pillar of Oinomaos
6 Temple of Hera
7 Stadium Track
8 Prytaneum
9 The Treasuries
10 Council House
(Dotted line indicates future site of Temple of Zeus)

Figure 5.1   Site of Olympia, about 525 BC

even a synonym – for peace seems to go back to ancient Olympia. Perhaps there is even some relevance in Pindar's notion of Hyperborea, where Herakles found the olive, as a land of continuous universal peace.

Apart from the Temple of Hera, which is dated about 600 BC, and a few of the "Treasuries" that were its near contemporaries, the earliest buildings were built about the mid-sixth century BC. They were the first phase of the *Bouleuterion*, or Council House, and the *Prytaneum*, a kind of Town Hall.

Besides any legislative powers that the Council might have had, it served as a court of appeals for decisions about the outcome of the athletic events. The makeup of the council is unknown, but presumably it consisted of at least one member from each of the tribes in the district. Because evidence is complicated by disputes, both ancient and modern, about who controlled the site, little is certain. But in early years the district which provided council members may have included the inhabitants of and near both Elis and Pisa. At some point all Council members became Elean, and Pisatans were left out.

Organization and Administration

The Council was overseen by the *Hellanodikai,* or "Judges of the Greeks," who were the principal organizers as well as the chief judges of the Olympic Games. In the early years there were only two *Hellanodikai,* perhaps one Pisatan, one Elean; later both were from Elis. Sometime in the fifth century BC the number was expanded to a board of nine administrator-judges, who divided among themselves responsibility for producing the various specific events of the games.

Although Olympia was not really a city, it possessed this ordinarily municipal building, the *Prytaneum* or Town Hall. The administrative offices were in the *Prytaneum,* which served other important functions. It contained the altar of Hestia, the Greek goddess of the hearth. There, officials maintained an Eternal Flame, which all local inhabitants could use for rekindling their home fires, if needed. In later years, at least, if the Eternal Flame itself ever went out, it was relit with solar energy rather than by an imported flame taken from a fire already burning elsewhere. This practice prompted a prominent traditional feature of the modern Olympics; namely, the lighting of the flame for the Olympic torch relay that travels from Olympia to the host city of a modern Olympiad. The flame for our torch relay, an innovation of the 1936 Berlin Olympics, is lit by solar power at the Temple of Hera, by a young Greek woman usually likened to an ancient priestess of Hestia (see appendix C). The ancient Town Hall provided still other vital services, most importantly as a banquet hall and reception center for various notable guests. It was also the site for the start of official religious festival processions, and other elements of the cult.

Athletes' entries would need the Olympic officials' approval. The procedure for obtaining it varied over the centuries. On this subject there is much modern confusion. Modern historians regularly state that thirty days' training at Elis was rigidly required of all prospective Olympic athletes before they could be authorized to compete in the actual festival. There is some reason to believe that such a thirty-day period was indeed demanded in the last phase of the games, during the Roman Empire. By then the Olympics had evolved for centuries and attracted hosts of aspiring athletes from all Greek-speaking sections of this late Greco-Roman world (see chapter 12). But the games that eventually burgeoned into the complex truly international games of that later immense Greco-Roman world indisputably began on a very small scale. If there was only one event at first and for several decades, the original 200 meter dash, no one would assert that the thirty-days' training rule was operative at that time.

There is no evidence for when this rule was introduced. The earliest reference to it dates from the second century AD, and even then it comes not from Pausanias, but from the notoriously unreliable Philostratus (*Life of Apollonius* 5.43). A few even later authors also mention a thirty-day rule, but that it was operative much earlier and applied to the famous athletes of Pindar's time seems highly unlikely. Some scholars point out that Elis was merely a district until 472, when an actual city of that name was founded. They suggest that the requirement that athletes train for thirty days in Elis could not have antedated the city itself. Some historians think it was inaugurated then. I myself doubt that it was even that early, and may well be centuries later; otherwise, I suspect, some author before Philostratus would have mentioned it. And there would be no need to detain busy professional men that long until the number of contestants became unmanageable otherwise.

Some basic administrative matters attested only in accounts of the thirty-day period necessarily took place much earlier, as well. The officials apparently employed the pre-tournament method that we call "seeding," that is, matching the better contestants against those less likely to succeed (Pausanias 6.23.2, 6.24.1). The intent of that kind of "seeding" is to avoid having one of the best athletes eliminated in an early match by another like him, while a mediocre contestant reaches a final round by luckily facing only athletes who are even worse. Seeding is especially useful in one-on-one elimination contests, such as tennis or the ancient combat events. For running events, there were what we call preliminary elimination "heats." Only the first or the first few finishers are permitted to advance to the next stage of the competition (Gardiner 1910: 205). By such means organizers insured that the number of lanes in the stadium track accommodated all the runners in the final race.

As soon as the boys' events were introduced in the latter part of the seventh century BC, the officials needed a preliminary session of some kind to determine age groups. If a specific applicant did not meet the standards for the younger division, he would be compelled to compete as a man. With no birth certificates, the officials made these decisions on the basis of their – literally arbitrary – judgment as to a contestant's maturity and probable age. In one case an applicant, the wrestler Nikasylos of Rhodes, was rejected as a boy, but he then won the men's division (Pausanias 6.14.1–2, with no hint of a date).

By the middle of the sixth century BC even more athletes and spectators were attending the games. Besides the archaeological evidence for expansion, such as the new buildings, there is the noticeable influx of competitors from Magna Graecia. Yet at this time the officials still would need nothing like thirty days for those preparatory activities, and I doubt that the athletes were required to spend thirty days just as proof of their "good faith." Nor, I suspect, would the *Hellanodikai* be eager to cover the expense of the athletes' board and room for so long a period just to ensure their dedication to the enterprise.

The Stone of Tantalus Averted

The first half of the fifth century BC is a crucial one for the history of Greece, even for the history of Western humankind. In 490 and again in 480 a large Persian army invaded Greece, seeking to subdue it and turn it into their vassal state. The invasion failed. Had the Persians succeeded in their attempt to conquer Greece, European life to this day would be markedly different. When and how the Americas and Australia would have been discovered and colonized is a fascinating but now wholly pointless question. A more practical, but still provocative, question is how the Greeks themselves could so cannily perceive the gravity of the Persian invasion and the importance of the war's outcome.

The poet Pindar (see chapter 6) deemed whether the Greeks won or lost a matter of no less than cosmic importance. Soon after the war, in a poem honoring a pancratiast, he compared the Persian threat to a mythological threat where Zeus – and with him the whole Greek way of life and the other gods – would be overthrown and replaced by some unknown, unruly god or monster. In Pindar's myth, Zeus averts his overthrow just as Greece managed to avoid being overcome by the Persian invaders. "Some god," the poet says, "has turned away the stone of Tantalus hanging over our heads, a burden utterly unbearable to Greece" (*Isthmian* 8.9–11; 26–47). The Stone of Tantalus is a mythological symbol for complete political subjugation and an end to all personal happiness. As a coincidental issue, I observe that no deities except the Olympian gods supported the practice of holding athletic competitions.

The favorable result of the war had a profound effect on Olympia and its games, while they, in turn, played a significant role in the experience of postwar Greece. The Greeks expelled their Persian enemy after the famous battles of Salamis in 480 BC and Plataea in 479 BC. The military effort and the victory had been truly Panhellenic. It was the first time so many Greek states had acted together as one. They were usually at war with one another, not with a common enemy. A Panhellenic spirit began to surge throughout the land, but most of all at Olympia, the very embodiment of Panhellenism. The next two Olympiads mark a special peak in Olympic history, when the festival and the games would nearly match their potential (Sinn 2000: 55; Gardiner 1910: 115–17).

Olympia Thrives, Greece Falters

More people flocked to Olympia than ever before, all in jubilation. Partly for a slightly different reason, Sinn even calls the games of 476 BC the "jubilation Olympics" (2000: 57). More contestants came, and the athletes of this period are among the best and best known in Greek history. More poets attended; Pindar's career was at its peak, and he composed several of his best victory odes at this point. Many others came, including notable politicians, such as Themistocles, who were prominent partly for their activities in the war. Most importantly, more donations came. Zeus' cult at Olympia was the happy recipient of many valuable donations, as people and states immediately began to dedicate their booty from the war to the god. Some donations were opulent; Olympia – and Elis – became affluent.

Many changes took place. The number of *Hellanodikai* was expanded from two to nine. There were so many pilgrims, athletes, and contests that the program of events itself could not be completed in the time allotted. Athletes were called to their matches after dark. So the number of days allowed for the festival and its contests was expanded, although exact details are not certain. The duration of the festival suddenly expanded from one or two days to four or five, according to most estimates.

In another major change the citizens of Elis built a "bricks and mortar" city. Previously, Elis was just a loose confederation of neighboring villages with no real center. Now those villagers built a center. The new city of Elis was planned from the start with its role as Olympic host in mind. There were at least two gymnasiums and space for a horse track in the center of town. The Eleans constructed a special permanent building where the new *Hellanodikai* could stay, as they did, for as many as ten months in the year before the games.

The most important innovation was unfortunately not permanent, but rather transitory. The Greeks decided Olympia was to end wars among them, and it was officially designated as the agent of peace. A significant number of cities agreed to allow the Olympic officials to form a kind of judicial appeals board which would allow disputing cities to settle their differences by arbitration instead of arms. The year was 476 BC.

For a while it actually worked. Archaeologists found on the site a sheet of bronze inscribed with the board's verdict in two specific cases. "Olympia became the symbol of harmony among all Greek states" (Sinn 2000: 56). Olympia long remained a *symbol* of peace in antiquity – and it still does now, I think. But its value soon became symbolic only, as it lost its power for peace. Within a few years the member states ceased to recognize the authority of the Olympic appeals board, and no longer submitted cases to it. And in just a few short decades, when those who planned the noble peace experiment in 476 BC had hoped they would be enjoying the fruits of a Panhellenic peace, the exact opposite reigned. All Greeks were at war with other Greeks.

Called the Peloponnesian War, it was probably one of the worst
wars, one of the most all-encompassing, one of the bloodiest and
cruelest in the history of humankind. Brutal atrocities of Greeks
on Greeks were common; and neither of the principal combatants,
Athens and Sparta, would tolerate neutrality from the others. To
choose peace was not an option (Thucydides 1.1). As suggested by
the brevity of the 476 BC Olympic pact for peace, many hostile
actions began to take place decades before the traditional dates of
this long war, namely, 431–404 BC.

Olympia, even at those times when Elis was drawn into the
conflict, fared better than most places. And that Golden Olympic
Decade of the 470s would leave a grand and permanent imprint on
the site and its institutions, and on Greece itself (Sinn 2000: 56).
Its success would eventually cause Olympia to become the biggest
tourist attraction in the ancient world. It triggered the making of
Zeus' new temple, and his new cult statue, which was judged one
of the Seven Wonders of the Ancient World. Therefore its fame still
extends into our own media and our children's schoolbooks.

As soon as it could, the suddenly wealthy Olympia began an ambitious building program in the 470s. The *Bouleuterion*, for example,
was doubled in size by the addition of another wing, exactly like
and parallel to the first one. New "Treasuries" were donated and
added to the others. A fine stone terrace was made below them.
These treasury buildings are not large, but their decorations, number,
location, and international character make them impressive. The
stadium was moved slightly, and both it and its spectator facilities
improved.

The focal point of it all was the new and justly renowned temple
of Olympian Zeus. Exactly when its construction began is not clear,
but the building was not completed until 456.[1] The architect was
Libon of Elis. This temple was immense. It was almost 30 meters
wide and more than 70 meters long; in height it reached about 21
meters. A golden statue of the goddess Nike ("Victory") crowned
its peak above the west pediment. The sculptures in the pediments
themselves merit some attention. The western pediment contained
a scene from a well-known myth, the battle between the Lapiths
and the Centaurs. The statues on the eastern pediment, on the
entrance end, represented the main myth of Olympia, Pelops' chariot

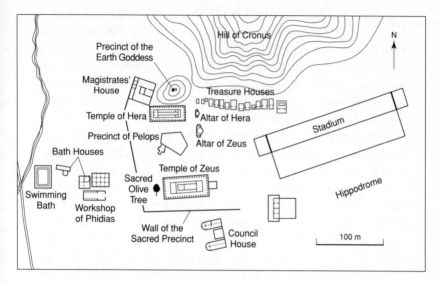

Figure 5.2 Site of Olympia, about 425 BC

race against Oinomaos. Zeus himself stands erect in its center. On his left stand Oinomaos and his wife; on his right, Pelops and Hippodameia, who was Oinomaos' daughter and eventually Pelops' bride. In the low, pointed corners at either end lie the two rivers, the Alpheus and the Cladeus, in anthropomorphic form. The scene on the pediment represents the moment before the race. The best-known version of this myth appears in Pindar's *Olympian* 1 (see chapter 6).

Behind the impressive vestibule was the spacious *cella*, the main religious sanctuary, where the great cult statue would later sit. Its entrance had an elaborate antechamber with pillars, bronze gates, and many smaller statues and dedications. The *cella* had two levels, with a staircase to an upper balcony, where pilgrims could eventually view Zeus' head in front of them, without having to look straight up at the towering god, as we might look at a modern skyscraper. Everything in the room was luxurious, impressive, and expensive.

Behind the *cella*, but entirely partitioned off, was the *opisthodomos*, "rear chamber," a room about the same size as the *cella*, but not nearly so lavish. From its exterior porch, speakers wanting attention could gather a large audience below them. The best-known case is Herodotus, who, from this back porch, read his *Histories* to the crowd as the means of their first publication. At least one famed painter, Zeuxis, saw Olympia as a place to gain good exposure for his work. Later, prominent philosophers, professors, and orators made their mark using the Olympics as a forum. The list is almost a Who's Who of ancient Greece.

Some famous visitors, over the centuries, were the orators Gorgias, Demosthenes, and Isocrates; and the philosophers Thales (who supposedly died there of the heat), Pythagoras, Empedocles, Anaxagoras, Plato, and Aristotle. The list includes many other notables, such as Themistocles, Aeschylus, Thucydides, and Alexander the Great. Not all of these presented their professional works when there, and the ancient sources which record some of these visits might be questioned as apocryphal. But there is no doubt that the Olympic Games were the best place in ancient Greece to see and be seen, to be heard and to hear. That role for Olympia is all the more noteworthy when one remembers how far away it was from the mainstream of Greek commercial traffic and personal travel.

Except for Pheidias' statue of the god, the most distinctive feature of Zeus' temple was probably its roof. It was composed of a material rarely, if ever, seen on a roof – tiles made of heavy marble. Furthermore, the marble used was not ordinary marble, but the finest, the most prized and most expensive of marbles; namely, that imported from the island of Paros. Because of the weight and the height of the roof, it required sophisticated engineering to keep it from collapsing immediately. It did not collapse. Its perimeter had a gutter with a marble lion's head atop each of 100 vertical pipes used as "down spouts."

The Seventh Wonder of the World

All this magnificence, however, took second place to the jewel of the temple, the jewel of Olympia, the statue of Zeus by the renowned Athenian sculptor Pheidias. He was considered the greatest Greek artist of all time by many people then, and many still. Although the temple itself was finished in 456 BC, Pheidias did not start his statue at Olympia until 437. He had long been occupied with a commission from Pericles to do various public works and especially the monumental statue of Athena, which stood more than 15 meters tall in the Parthenon on the Athenian Acropolis. When he finished his Athena there in 438, he promptly moved to Olympia, where his commission allowed him a large expense account for materials and numerous assistants. His own fee was also very high (Drees 1968: 146).

The officials immediately built a tall and spacious separate building for him to work in. This building, the Workshop of Pheidias, has been well investigated by the archaeologists. They found remarkable evidence of his personal presence there, including some stone pieces with which he practiced in preparing for the real thing. An especially intriguing discovery is a clay cup, datable to exactly the right time, bearing the inscription "Property of Pheidias." It is plainly a cup that the famed sculptor put to his lips.

As with the Athena in the Parthenon, the specifications he was given made the statue so large that both traditional mediums, marble and cast bronze, were out of the question because of their weight. As at Athens, Pheidias solved the difficulty by using gold and ivory instead. Their choice was perhaps as much for practical reasons as for their aesthetic impression and appeal. By overlaying a large wooden framework with gold and ivory plates he could make a statue so light that despite its size it would not crumble or break with its own weight. But it was heavy even as it was. The gold alone in Pheidias' somewhat comparable Athena Parthenos on the Acropolis weighed well over a ton, according to Pericles as quoted by Thucydides (2.13.5). Both statues obviously contained an immense fortune in gold, to say nothing of their ivory and artistic merits.

Naturally, both the building of the wooden substructure and the shaping of the plates to attach to it required truly rare artistic and engineering skills. In order to protect the wood from rotting, Pheidias – or one of his chief assistants – devised a system of pipes that, when activated, would carry oil to the wood. An injection of oil, even at infrequent intervals, kept the wood from rotting for more than seven centuries. The oil helped to preserve the ivory, as well. Although the statue was nearly 20 meters high, it represented a seated Zeus; he was on his throne. The seated position not only complicated the framework and lubrication system; it also required that body parts, in particular the head, be larger (and heavier) than in a standing version of the same height (figure 5.3).

The greatest problems which the artist faced were those of perspective; how to make a statue so large viewable from various angles, and from both the main floor and the upper gallery. It is not overstatement to say that his success was phenomenal. Coins which bear the statue's image convey some idea of what it looked like. Pausanias, along with many others, gives an elaborate description (5.11.1–10). All such descriptions and the lore attached to the statue make the ancient comments about it sound overly hyperbolic to our ears. But the ancient authors are so lavish in their praise, so obviously full of genuine awe, that the hyperbolic transforms into the authentic and believable. Pausanias (5.11.9) says that, on seeing the statue, he could not believe the official measurements; he thought it appeared much bigger than reports about it claimed. To judge from others' reactions to Pheidias' masterpiece, that first seemingly hyperbolic statement must be true. I refer to Pausanias' suggestion that no description, even if factually accurate, could adequately convey the impression the statue made on its viewers. One needed to see the statue for oneself in order to appreciate it. Unfortunately, that we can never do.

In the light of ancient viewers' comments, it is no wonder that Pheidias' statue was prominent in the list of the Seven Wonders. Even during the Roman Empire, visitors Greek, Roman, and from elsewhere agree with earlier generations, that this particular statue was the greatest achievement in the entire course of Greek art. I give just a brief sampling and summary paraphrase of a few comments:

> It is the most holy and the most beautiful statue in the whole world.
> It is the actual manifestation of the deity.
> The beauty of the statue is so great that it seems itself to add something to Greek religion.
> Either Zeus descended from heaven or Pheidias ascended to it for a first-hand look.
> It is a calamity if one dies without having seen the statue of Zeus in Olympia.[2]

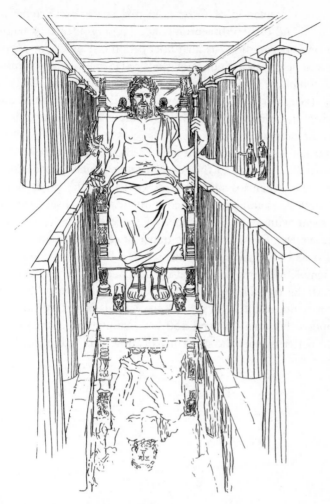

Figure 5.3 Pheidias' statue of Zeus

The temple of Zeus and its gold and ivory cult statue are obviously in Pausanias' mind when he prefaces his report about them by saying that the Olympic Games have been blessed with "a unique share of divine thought" (5.10.1). The statue was not finished until 433, in the midst of decades of turmoil and almost on the eve of the official Peloponnesian War. The statue, when finished, was already a relic of another age. It was clearly the somewhat belated symbolic culmination of those golden days of the Olympics, the late sixth and early fifth centuries BC. Those golden days had had their own apex in the 470s, that brief period of Panhellenic cooperation and celebration right after the Persian menace was removed. "The temple of Zeus was truly a national memorial of the Persian wars" (Gardiner 1910: 119). It was then that the Eleans began to build the temple of Zeus, even if the statue was completed in very different circumstances.

Pheidias' great statue of Athena Parthenos was short-lived, unfortunately a casualty of the war. Needing capital to continue the effort, the Athenians melted it down to get the gold. But the temple of Zeus and its renowned statue at Olympia survived, bearing silent witness to the temper of those glorious earlier times. They survived for an amazing number of centuries, right up to the final years of the games (see chapter 12). But both the statue and the temple are now obliterated by time. There still survives, however, to this day, a living witness to the spirit of those golden times, and it is not silent even yet. Most of Pindar's victory odes were composed between 490 and 460 BC. Nothing either then or now could better capture the mentality of those truly exceptional days.

6

Pindar and Immortality

Pindar's Place in Literature and Los Angeles

It is not mere chance that the best evidence for the Olympics, even for Greek athletics in general, comes from precisely that period of exceptional glory; namely, the last few decades of the sixth century BC and the first few decades of the fifth, especially the 470s. These were the days of the "big name" athletes of antiquity. Because many ancient authors, even apart from Pindar, seem to concentrate on them, the sources identify more athletes from those times than any other, and there is more elaborate information about them as individuals (Golden 1998: 86). The lone papyrus scrap that preserves a bit of Hippias' list of all the victors, Olympiad by Olympiad, not just those from the 200 meters, covers the years 480 to 448 (see chapter 2). Most of the vases bearing athletic scenes come from the second half of the sixth and first half of the fifth centuries BC. Athletic subjects became less and less popular after that, and such vases mostly disappeared by the fourth century BC.

The days of the *epinician* were even more concentrated. An *epinician* or victory ode was a poem commissioned by a victorious athlete or someone on his behalf to praise the winner and to celebrate his success. It was a choral poem, set to music, which a singing and dancing chorus ordinarily performed at the athlete's victory party, although a few had other settings. For a fee, the commissioned poet wrote the lyrics and probably the music. Normally, he himself would train the chorus, composed of the athlete's fellow citizens, for the first performance. But the poem was not a momentary item. The text was preserved, and probably given one or more repeat performances by the athlete, his family, or his native city. And, in the ancient sense, it was published; that is, copies were distributed to anyone the victor or poet wished to have them. Or, whoever wanted a copy would obtain one from the victor or poet. After such a start, the new poem could enter the body of Greek literature and take a respected place alongside poems of other types, such as the great epics, or the public hymns for the gods, which these same *epinician* poets also composed.

The victory ode did not last long as a living genre. Virtually all the poems known can be dated between the waning years of the sixth century BC and the mid-fifth; and they come from just three authors.[1] The best known is Pindar. The others are Simonides and Bacchylides, Pindar's slightly older and slightly younger contemporaries, respectively.

More than a dozen of Bacchylides' victory odes were recovered – in a somewhat tattered state – by the sensational discovery at the end of the nineteenth century of a papyrus almost two millennia old. No complete poem of Simonides survived the neglect of the Middle Ages. We have only snippets of his work, preserved by other ancients who quote him. That is doubly unlucky. First, if he did not create the genre, he was the first to make it in demand. Second, those snippets are truly impressive; even the ancients judged him as one of the very best Greek poets, perhaps second only to Pindar, whom they ranked first.

Pindar's *Epinician Odes* are the *only* complete lyric poems that survived the Middle Ages in manuscript form. They were resuscitated in the Renaissance, when such manuscripts were found and published. Pindar's poems now occupy a prominent position among the standard works of Greek literature, such as Homer, Sophocles, or Plutarch. Almost a fourth of Pindar's work is preserved. Luckily for us, that fourth consists of his victory odes. Forty-five complete *epinicians* are extant, most of them about 100 lines long, divided into four "books." In length, a "book" of an ancient author compares with what we call a chapter. These four books are Pindar's collected *epinicians* for athletes who won in the Olympian, Pythian, Nemean, and Isthmian Games, respectively, and the books bear the names of those festivals.

The first poem in the collection, headed by the book of *Olympians*, is called *Olympian* 1. It begins by proclaiming that the Olympics outshine all the others as the sun outshines all other stars at noon (see chapter 2). The Big Four games were ranked in a hierarchy of importance, and the Olympics topped the list. Nevertheless – and the point must be stressed – Pindar's outlook toward athletes and the meaning of their victories does not vary at all from festival to festival. The last *Isthmian* has the same purpose as the first *Olympian*, the same universal purport, and the same importance in expressing the value and potential of a victory. In interpreting Pindar's poetry, critics do not regard passages in the *Olympians* as any more important, by virtue of their location, than those in other books.

Pindar, a native of Thebes, lived from about 518 to 438 BC. These and many of the dates which scholars assign to his poems are somewhat uncertain, but cannot be far from the mark. He wrote his first *epinician* about 498, his last, about 446 BC. The biographical details which appear in some later authors are mostly pure speculation, and we know almost nothing about his personal life. But his ideas are, one might say, an open book.

Despite Pindar's lofty reputation for quality, critics ancient and modern traditionally regard him as the most difficult of all Greek authors. His style is always extremely compressed, often allusive rather than explicit, sometimes even crabbed, and usually brilliant – worth the effort, most of us think. And he can tell us much about ancient athletics, especially about the meaning of the competition and the value of victory. He ties those things, however, inextricably to the value of poetry, his favorite topic. He identifies three themes to illustrate the unique powers of his poetry. They are the themes of *permanence, mobility*, and *vocal/verbal communication*.

The temple and statue of Zeus at Olympia were preserved for more than seven centuries (see chapter 5), before they disappeared or crumbled away (see chapter 12). Pindar's position views that as not long enough – he can do better, he believes, and he has. He once compares his poem to one of those seemingly permanent treasury buildings at the sanctuary, of which the primary function, as the name suggests, was preservation. Pindar says that he has made for the victor:

> a plentiful treasure house of song. Neither the invading rainstorm, a pitiless army sent by the thunder and clouds, nor its wind will batter and carry *this* treasury into the sea-depths along with the debris that carries everything along with it. (*Pythian* 6.7–14)

Pindar also contrasts the stationary nature of statues, such as those of the victors, with the mobility of his song:

> I am not a sculptor, so as to execute figures which stand motionless in one place. Rather on every ship large and small, sweet song, sail from Aegina and spread the word that Pytheas, the powerful son of Lampon, has been crowned victor in the *pancration*. (*Nemean* 5.1–5)

Finally, he contrasts one of his poems, "a talking memorial-stone," as he calls it, with an ordinary memorial-stone, which is a silent witness of few words (*Nemean* 8.44–8).

In the overflowing Los Angeles Coliseum, at the closing ceremony of Olympiad 23 in 1984, the final item was a reading by the noted actor Richard Basehart. Not only was it the last moment of these Olympics, it was also the last reading Basehart ever gave; he died shortly thereafter. His quotation comes from the last poem ever written by the author – Pindar.

> Creatures of a Day! Man is merely a shadow of a dream.
> But when god-given glory comes upon him in victory,
> a bright light shines upon us,
> and our life is sweet.
> [When the end comes, the loss of flame brings darkness;
> but his glory is bright forever].
> *Pythian* 8.95–7
> (The words in square brackets are not in Pindar but were added for
>   the closure of the games and termination of the Olympic flame
>   in Los Angeles. Further, the word translated "glory" literally
>   means "gleam.")

Through his poem, composed 2,500 years earlier, Pindar managed to star at those Olympics in Los Angeles. He provided their climax. Obviously, in one sense, he was not wholly dead. His appearance – by way of this poem – in California in 1984 itself illustrates those three themes explained above, the *mobility*, the *permanence*, and the *vocal/verbal nature* of his poetry of praise. Pindar naturally stresses how poetry will benefit the athletic victors whom he celebrates. In the case of the poem in question, that victor is a wrestler named Aristomenes. Yet neither the poet nor the athlete would have the benefit of the endurance of their names, if people had not thought the poem worth preserving as literature, had not seen in it something of lasting value to humankind.

Something like the Gods

How can it be, one must naturally ask, that Western tradition thought Pindar's poems for wrestlers worth saving, while it allowed all other lyric poets to disappear wholly. Part of the answer is the excellence of Pindar's poetry, which does not emerge in translation. Although Pindar's own public hymns for the gods perished, why was a poem for a wrestler preserved? And if he was the greatest lyric poet antiquity had, why did Pindar spend his talents writing for wrestlers and runners? There are answers. In our society, a great gulf ordinarily separates our world of serious literature from our world of athletics. That is not true of Pindar's times or of the nature of his *epinicians*.

For Pindar, the athletic contest served as a microcosm of the general human struggle to pass beyond ordinary human limitations, to effect extraordinary achievements, to do something that humans cannot ordinarily do. Modern writers often stress that the Olympic Games were attached to a religious festival in honor of the god Zeus. They then assert that the athletes went to Olympia as worshippers and somehow viewed their athletic competition as a religious act. But that notion is all wrong. The attachment of the games to the religious festival makes the competitions an act of religious devotion no more than the attachment of a modern "big-time" college football game to a university makes it an act of education.

As college football began as spare-time diversion for college students, and grew into something vastly different, the Olympics may well have begun with contests among the pilgrims who had come to take part in the cult of Zeus. But all pertinent evidence suggests that by the early sixth century BC, when the athletic circuit was formed, if not earlier, religion is not what drew athletes to Olympia, even if they actively participated in the public religious ceremonies. Money no doubt was a factor. Victors could win no prize of value at Olympia itself, but to win there was a "ticket," so to speak, to high profit from other sources (see chapter 8).

For the best athletes, however, money alone is never the only, or even the main, incentive; rather, it is the urge to compete, to do one's best, to win at the highest level against others at the highest level – those were the athletes' main motives in coming to Olympia.[2] Closely related are pride, glory, and fame – they all play a role. Even returning victors hoped to win again and to add to their résumés, or even to set a record, and to have their names associated with the best possible achievements.

To say that Olympic competition was an act far more secular than religious is *not* to say that the Greeks thought athletic competition had no connection with the gods. The poem from which Basehart read calls victory "the god-given glory" ("gleam"). Pausanias believed that "a unique share of divine thought" had been bestowed on Olympia (5.10.1; see chapter 5). Elsewhere, Pindar declares, "There is a divine presence in a judgment of human strength." The last sentence needs its context:

> In athletic games the victor wins the glory his heart desires
> as crown after crown is placed on his head,
> when he wins with his hands or swift feet.
> *There is a divine presence in a judgment of human strength.*
> Only two things, along with prosperity, advance life's sweetest prize:
>   if a man has success and then gets a good name. *Don't expect*
>   *to become Zeus.* You have everything
>   if a share of these two blessings comes your way.
> *Isthmian* 5.8–15

This key passage contains so many of Pindar's major themes that we must return to it several times in the following pages.

Elsewhere, in a very similar context, Pindar nearly repeats the sentence "Don't expect to become Zeus": "Don't seek to become a god" (*Olympian* 5.24). Sometimes modern critics say that the Greeks regarded their Olympic victors as gods. Of course, that is nonsense.[3] Pindar is not admonishing his athletes or warning them not to think along those lines. Rather, he is giving them the very highest possible praise. As he expresses it, they have done everything. They have reached such a high state that there is nothing left for them. They have already reached the pinnacle of human achievement.

There are in Pindar's work a few other versions of the same theme, but not focused on the question of becoming a god. Overall it probably occurs about a dozen times. Pindaric scholars call the theme the "*ne plus ultra*" motif, Latin for "No more beyond." In a popular tale, others, not Pindar, applied an even more extreme version of this extreme theme to the boxer Diagoras (see chapter 7).

The *ne plus ultra* idea, however, cuts both ways. Besides being the highest praise the poet can give, it is also an obvious reminder of human limitations. No one is perfect, or can "have it all" forever. Another passage begins by emphasizing the negative side of the issue:

> The race of men is one thing, that of the gods, is another.
> There is a total difference in power, so that we are nothing –
> while the bronze heaven remains the gods' secure seat forever.
> But, nevertheless – *we can become something like the gods*,
> through *excellence* – excellence of *mind or* of *body*;
> even if we don't know from day to day – or night to night –
> what finish line fate has marked for our run.
> *Nemean* 6.1–7

Capturing the Moment

Pindar emphasizes mortals' dismal performance compared to that of the eternal gods. Compared to them, we are absolutely nothing. The gods are permanent and perfect. We mortals are neither. We all know that to err is human; but outright incompetence is far from uncommon. And when we die, it is worse than incompetence. It is an absolute failure. As with Basehart's "man is a shadow of a dream" quotation from *Pythian* 8, these comments are about as pessimistic as is possible. But also, as in the other passage, the pessimism functions mainly to draw a contrast with the approaching positive evaluation of high achievement. "But nevertheless," Pindar continues – there are two words for "but" – "*But nevertheless* we can become *something like* the immortal gods through *excellence*, excellence of mind *or* of body."

Despite our generally mistake-prone, even bumbling nature, there are moments when humans perform at an excellent level. Occasionally we do something of extremely high quality. Yet rarely do people achieve something of such high quality that it amazes, seems almost beyond human capabilities. That is when we are something like the gods; and that accomplishment can occur in any sphere, mental or physical, or any other. All acts of true human excellence – so long as that excellence is truly extraordinary – are like the divine. Yet there is a difficulty here.

The athlete's performance, the excellence which he displays, may be like that of the immortal gods, but the athlete who performs it is not a god. Far from it; as Pindar puts it, "we are nothing"; there is nothing permanent about us. But what Pindar offers his victor-patrons is a means to capture that transitory moment "when the god-given glory comes, and the bright light shines" upon him, in the words heard in Los Angeles, and to make it permanent; to make his athletes' achievements immortal even if he cannot do the same for the athletes themselves.

The only way to make the moment of glory permanent in Pindar's time and in his mind is to have the moment preserved in literature. In *Nemean* 7 he again terms the athlete's victory a "success," a worthy subject for song. The passage continues: "Great acts of valor receive only darkness if they lack songs. There is only one way that we know to hold a mirror to noble deeds; namely, if they find compensation in songs of glory through Memory, mother of the Muses" (11–16).

The phrase "receive darkness" clearly means "be forgotten," "not survive." The same notion occurs in *Olympian* 10, when Pindar expresses it more boldly and even baldly: "Whenever a man has wrought deeds of excellence without song, he goes down to the Underworld having provided little delight for all his toil. He has breathed in vain" (91–3).

The theme of "immortality" through poetry permeates all of Pindar's *epinicians*, and it is the major theme of *Pythian* 3. The poet contrasts medicine and poetry in their capacity to preserve a person. To pursue immortality through medicine is futile, for it must ultimately fail. Literature cannot fully succeed, but as proof of its partial success, at least, Pindar points to some heroes from the Trojan War, who lived centuries before his time. "We still know of Nestor and Sarpedon, and talk about them, because of the glorifying words expressed by the craftsmen of song" (112–14). He appeals to the present knowledge of the past as proof that the future will know of the present. And he compares his poetry to the medical art elsewhere: "When the decision is made, the best healers of pains and toil are celebration and songs; praise linked to the lyre soothes the limbs better than warm water. *The word lives longer than the deeds*" (*Nemean* 4.1–6).

The concluding passage of *Nemean* 8 confesses: "To bring your soul back again, Megas, that I cannot do." But Pindar soon adds that he can send up a cheer in praise of the athlete's victory, and "render even great toil painless" through the medicine of song. He again appeals to events from the distant past and the heroes of Greek myth, who still live on in song: "There were songs of praise long, long ago, even before Adrastus and the Thebans fought" (44–54).

The Poet of Myth

Pindar sometimes compares his victor-patrons themselves to the heroes of Greek mythology. By itself, neither the past nor the present implies a general truth. But by holding his contemporaries up against individuals famous through myth, Pindar affirms the permanence of that past by its continuing relevance to the present. Conversely, by referring his own subjects to examples from the distant past, he validates their participation in a recognized, lasting pattern of human life. The comparison is rarely explicit, often just clearly implied. Several victors in combative events are presented as parallels to heroes of myth known mostly for their exploits on the battlefield. Rarely, however, is the implied comparison a direct one-to-one similarity. It is often more complex than that, and frequently not an individual but something else which Pindar sees in his and his patron's world as similar to something told of the past. And many of the comparisons are so elaborate that they are clothed in an extended narrative of a myth.

Pindar's skill as a myth-teller is even a major part of his poetic reputation. Because his best-known myths are so long and elaborate, I focus here only on the one most relevant to the Olympic Games. The hero Pelops had a hero shrine in the *Altis* close to the altar of Zeus (see chapters 2 and 5), and the major myth about him concerns his chariot race with King Oinomaos on the future site of Olympia. A few ancient sources even regard this race as the very origin of the Olympic Games. Pindar himself makes no such claim, but clearly implies that this fabled race is pertinent to the early history of Olympia.

The Pelops myth appears as the long central section of *Olympian* 1, more than a half of this rather extensive poem. *Olympian* 1 celebrates the equestrian victory won in 476 BC by Hieron, the powerful and wealthy monarch of Syracuse, Sicily, which was one of the most populous and important cities in the Mediterranean world at that time. Pindar, perhaps purposely, leaves several details of his version obscure, and critics still strongly pursue and dispute them. He embarks on this lengthy narrative by proclaiming that Hieron's glory "shines out from the adopted land of Pelops." Some moderns might find the beginning of the story that follows somewhat offensive, but few Greeks would have shared that feeling. Pindar says that the god Poseidon fell in love with Pelops and on his golden chariot carried him up to Mount Olympus to be the gods' waiter and his own lover.

Later, Pelops' father, Tantalus, whom the gods had invited to dinner on Olympus, sinned by stealing and giving to his human friends the gods' nectar and ambrosia "with which the gods had made him immortal." Tantalus himself, now immortal, received eternal punishment, and his son was ejected from Mount Olympus back to earth and humankind. The young Pelops, now wanting to marry, moved from his native Lydia, in Asia Minor, to the north-western Peloponnesus, in order to court the young woman of his choice. She was Hippodameia, daughter of Oinomaos, king of Pisa and the area later called Olympia. But to court Hippodameia was to risk one's life, because her father required that the successful suitor must beat him in a chariot race. If the suitor lost, Oinomaos, almost by agreement, killed him. Thirteen suitors before Pelops had perished, but the young son of Tantalus resolved to try anyway.

Knowing the danger, Pelops called upon Poseidon to help him in return for the favors he had previously given the god. Poseidon responded by supplying his own chariot and magic horses. With these, Pelops won the race, killed Oinomaos, and indeed married Hippodameia. He also gained control of the whole area, and Peloponnesus literally means "Pelops' island." Pindar continues, "He now has his hero cult beside Zeus' altar at Olympia, and many visit his shrine and sacrifice to him." In words that recall the myth's beginning, when *Hieron*'s glory "shines out" from Olympia, Pindar then declares that *Pelops*' "glory shines out" from the Olympic track, where the athletic events are held. "And the victor has for the rest of his life sweet smooth sailing *because of the Games.*"

The above account omits much of this complex Pelops myth. Yet it should present the details needed to grasp references to Pelops' role at Olympia. Similarly, *Olympian* 1 as a whole is very elaborate and intricate, perhaps the poem on which Pindar worked the most, almost in proportion to Hieron's importance in the ancient world. It is the poem which opens by noting the supremacy of the Olympics over the others, as the sun is supreme in the sky. The poem is so intricate that an attempt to explain its meaning would require another chapter. *Olympian* 1 was, however, and is still, universally admired by those who can read it; one ancient author called it "the most beautiful of poems" (Lucian, *Somnium* 7).

Pindar's Summary of Pindar

I end this chapter with the somewhat shorter myth of *Nemean* 10, for I believe that it condenses most of Pindar's main argument into one rather brief story. In this poem, celebrating the victory of a wrestler named Theaios, the mythological narrative occupies the final section of the poem instead of the usual central portion. Perhaps that unusual position helps to explain its meaning.

The story concerns the two brothers, Castor and Pollux, also called the Dioscuri or "Sons of Zeus." They are also known as the patron gods of athletics, and were themselves highly skilled in some athletic events. In the myth told here, the Dioscuri get involved in a dispute over cattle rustling with another set of brothers, Idas and Lynkeus, and engage them in battle. Idas deals Castor a mortal blow. Pollux, full of grief, shouts out to Zeus, asking to die along with his beloved brother.

To Pollux' great surprise, Zeus actually answers, and informs him that Castor, who is in the throes of death, had a human father and is mortal. But, the god continues, he himself, Zeus, fathered him, Pollux. There was already such a version of the myth, in which their mother, Leda, had spent part of a night with Zeus, another part with her husband, Tyndareus. Zeus tells Pollux, as his son, that he can become ageless and deathless, and live happily for eternity with the rest of the gods on Mount Olympus.

In a startling and original twist to the myth, *not* part of any version before Pindar, Zeus then offers his son an amazing alternative to immortality. It is his destiny indeed to live forever with the rest of the gods – *unless he chooses otherwise*. Zeus then sets forth the rules: if Pollux really cares so much about his brother, he can share his own happy, immortal fate with his dying human brother, but only half of it. And he must then accept half of *Castor*'s fate as *his* own. If he prefers that to immortal bliss, he and Castor can be together always, but they must be dead on alternate days, living one day on Olympus, the next in the Underworld.

It is an amazing and arresting choice: immortality or dying truly countless times. Yet Pollux does not ponder nor hesitate. He makes his choice by action rather than words. "With no hesitation, first Pollux opened the eyes, then the voice of bronze-armored Castor." He restores his fallen brother to life – by reversing the act which every Greek was obligated to grant a newly deceased loved one. That duty was to close the eyes and the mouth, which were – and still are – often left open and disturbingly agape after a person dies (Homer, *Odyssey* 11.424–5; 24.292–4; Plato, *Phaedrus* 118).

Because this ritual and cosmetic act plays an important role in Greek culture, any Greek would recognize the effect of what Pollux does. Pindar never makes the commonplace statement, "He brought Castor back to life." Rather, it is the master touch of the master poet to take a common event and invert it in order to express the commonplace in a novel and compelling way, with a new significance. Castor's audible voice seals the finality of Pollux' choice and of the ambiguous future which the two brothers now enter.

End of poem. The entire *epinician* ends right there, with Pollux' decision and Castor's voice. At first one naturally wonders why Pindar would end a poem of praise in such an offbeat key. Usually the myth occupies a central position, and after telling the tale, the poet returns to the present, specifically to praise of his patron's victory and related matters, in what Pindaric scholars call the "Second Praise." Why is there no "Second Praise" here? The answer no doubt is Pindar's wish to stress the Dioscuri's double existence.

By appropriating the position of the Second Praise the myth assumes its function as well; that is, it praises the victor. By ending this way, Pindar implies that his victor-patrons at least *approach* the status of the model athletic heroes. He makes them half-immortal. Castor and Pollux can never truly become gods, but they still pass well beyond the ordinary human condition. So this half-immortality symbolizes the product of the interaction of poet and patron. Often drawn to questions of mortality and immortality, here Pindar gives us a myth which summarizes his main point – by blurring the line between the two conditions.

7

Body, Mind, and
Greek Athletics

Plato: "A Great Athlete"?

Most sports historians, classicists – and the modern Olympic movement – idealize the athletic system of ancient Greece, rating it
superior to our own. Typical are these remarks of Avery Brundage,
long the president of the IOC, who still defines much of our
Olympic thinking:

> In the enlightened "Golden Age," true culture was well rounded,
> requiring both physical and mental training. Philosophers, drama-
> tists, poets, sculptors and athletes met on common ground. Plato,
> the great thinker, was also a great athlete and won honors in the
> games . . . There was truly a marriage of fine arts and sport! Man
> probably more nearly realized that proud and happy condition of a
> sound mind in a sound body than ever before or since. (Brundage
> n.d.: 23)

These are the buzzwords: "both physical and mental training,"
"well rounded," and especially "a sound mind in a sound body."
Pierre de Coubertin, who founded the IOC in 1894, spoke of
"a happy balance": "*Mens sana in corpore sano*, as the ancients used
to say" (1986: 1.151 [1887]). Coubertin left the phrase "a sound
mind in a sound body" in its original Latin. One often reads these
words, in either language, in many books about the Olympics, and
hears them at meetings of Olympic or academic organizations.

People treat the phrase as somehow being a dictum or motto containing the philosophy of the ancient Olympic Games. They do not ask why Greek athletes spoke Latin, not Greek. There is, in fact, no evidence whatsoever in Greek (or Latin) literature to uphold the popular idea of the ancient Olympic athlete who is highly trained and proficient intellectually, as well.

Of the thousand or so known Olympic and Pythian victors, not *one* was ever noted for any intellectual achievement. And no Greek prominent in the intellectual world ever won a major athletic victory. Brundage does not specify in which games the "great athlete" Plato "won honors." But his source, the classicist E. N. Gardiner, names them: "Plato won victories in wrestling at Delphi, Nemea, and the Isthmus, and is even stated, with less probability, to have won the Olympic crown" (1930: 128). The vague "is even stated to have" is not technically false, for there is such a statement written in the Greek language. But there is no chance whatsoever that either it or Gardiner's assertion based on it is true. Decades ago more recent and more careful scholarship proved beyond doubt that both were ridiculously false (Rudolph 1974: 1475–7).

It is still a rather common modern belief that the great philosopher Plato was also a great athlete, and thus actually illustrates the ancient Olympic ideal of combining both physical and mental excellence. In order to dispel so misleading a belief, I here examine its evidence. This critique will also well illustrate the principles stated in chapter 2, above; namely, that any ancient statement must survive scrutiny. And its reliability is usually directly disproportionate to its chronological distance from the event which it reports. This comedy of errors goes like this. Plato says he often wrestled at his local gym. Some Plato fan turned that into "Plato was a first-rate wrestler."

Although there is a slightly earlier version in Latin, the first relevant accounts in Greek come from the third century AD. Then, more than five hundred years after Plato's death, two notoriously uncritical and unreliable authors state: "Plato was so good that some people say he even participated in the Isthmian games."

So far no one has yet claimed that Plato actually won a victory at any of the Big Four athletic games. Rather, they report that "some people" say that he "participated" in one of them. Even much later, nearly a millennium after Plato's death, a foolish early mediaeval author wrote a "tabloid" style biography of Plato, full of sensational, even supernatural events. This inventive biographer turns those earlier tentative reports of Plato's Isthmian participation into a certain claim that he won an "Isthmian, Pythian, maybe even Olympic victory." Gardiner, still our main source but often an uncritical scholar himself, took that bait. He has thus misled nearly a century of readers, while proving how far from the truth a story may "snowball" when passed through the mouths or pens of many people for many centuries.

Plato was not the only celebrated ancient writer to be credited also with exceptional athletic achievements. A similar early mediaeval and fanciful biography of Euripides assigns to the famous tragedian a boxing victory in the Panathenaic Games in Athens. A nineteenth-century French author read about this biography, but changed Euripides to "an Olympic victor." Coubertin was thus misled to say "Euripides was a champion boxer" (1986: 2.35 [1922]). The image of Euripides as a boxing champion at Olympia is worse than ridiculous; it is almost inconceivably absurd. But there it is in print, written by the man purported to be the founder of the modern Olympic movement.

As there is no specific case of a Greek who combined athletic with intellectual achievement, in all of ancient literature not a word is found that would support, even in the abstract, this supposed concept of the well-rounded topflight athlete who is a scholar as well. All evidence suggests that in Greek society the top athletes and top intellectuals were as clearly divided as they are in ours. Had we been reading the real Plato, instead of mediaeval *Lives* of Plato, we would have known that. I quote from Plato's *Laws* (807C): "An athlete who aims at Olympic or Pythian victory – he has *no* free time for anything else." That is, he must train full time. The same limitation applies to the so-called student-athletes in major American universities. If they aim at a national championship in football or basketball – or a career in professional sports – they must devote themselves full time to those goals. They have no time for anything else, such as serious academic work, to say nothing of superior academic achievement. The *very* few exceptions, most of them half a century or more ago, just prove the rule.

Body and Mind

Although the image of the Greek intellectual athlete proves to be pure myth, and a pernicious one, Greek literature may still teach us much about "body and mind" in Greek thought. There are hundreds of passages that touch on the topic, but here we will just observe some milestones along the way. Greek authors' attitudes toward the relationship of body and mind were not constant. Rather, they changed drastically over the centuries, preparing the way for the end of ancient athletics and for mediaeval Christianity's "hatred of the flesh." And the later authors are partly responsible for many of the problems in our own world of sport.

Homer often speaks in clear doublets, such as "on the battlefield and in counsel" or "in words and in deeds." But he never links body and mind, physical and mental; for they are not clearly delimited entities for Homer. Yet his mythological Odysseus, far more than any historical Greek, seems to excel both ways. Odysseus' unusual mental capacity is emphasized by his frequent stratagems and by his epithets, such as "with many thoughts" (*polymetis*). Yet he wins the foot race in *Iliad* 23, and far surpasses all the other discus throwers in *Odyssey* 8. It was there that Homer made the memorable statement, "So long as a man lives, he has no/greater glory than what he wins/with his feet or his hands in the games" (*Odyssey* 8.147–8; see chapter 1).

In the early fifth century BC, Pindar represents the mainstream of Archaic attitudes when he ranks physical/athletic excellence and mental/intellectual excellence all on the same high plane. The key passage in *Nemean* 6 was quoted above. There Pindar first noted mortals' dismal performance compared to that of the eternal gods. "But," Pindar continued, "*But* we can become something like the immortal gods through greatness, greatness of *mind or* greatness of *body*" (see chapter 6).

When we rise above ordinary human limitations and perform at a truly superlative level, almost perfect, and approach the divine, it can be in any category where the gods are perfect. It can be in body *or* in mind, physical excellence or mental excellence. Pindar does not prefer or rank one over the other. The gods are flawless, obviously weak neither in body nor in mind. Therefore *all* forms of human excellence, so long as they are truly of the highest order, are like the divine and can never be second rate, because nothing divine is second rate. Other passages in Pindar confirm this view. Though hardly expected to be found in one and the same person, both physical and mental excellence approach the divine and therefore both must always be equally treasured. That, I think, was the prevailing view in Archaic and early Classical Greece, the golden age of Greek athletics.

Body versus Mind

Almost from the beginning, there was a minority view, which looked at the athlete and his position in Greek society with strong disapproval. The philosopher Xenophanes lived well over ninety years and published his thoughts over more than seventy years, so we cannot date his remarks quoted below relative to the invention of the epinician victory ode, which took place in his lifetime. But what he says in the following denunciation of athletic glory certainly antedates Pindar's assertion of the potentially supreme glory of an athletic victory in *Nemean* 10, the poem with which chapter 6 closed. Xenophanes' purpose is to downgrade an Olympic victory and physical achievements and to claim that intellectual achievements are superior.

> If a man wins victory at Olympia/with the speed of his feet, in
>   wrestling or
> boxing, in the pentathlon or pancration/his fellow citizens look
>   up to him
> in awe. He is given a prominent seat of honor at public games,
> and, at public expense, he receives free board and a large gift,
> which would be a treasure for him. He would get all those things,
> *yet he is not as worthy as I am.*
> For *my wisdom is better* than the strength of humans or horses
> *It just is not fair to rank strength above my wisdom.*

What the philosopher belittles first is just what Homer praised first in *Odyssey* 8.147–8, above: glory won "with his *feet* or his hands."

And one can detect a bit of a whining tone when Xenophanes complains about the injustice of a system and culture that would rank physical strength over wisdom. It is probably true that many cities gave an athlete who won any of the Big Four games front row seats at all public events, and lifetime free board at public expense. And some gave a large lump sum "prize," probably a cash reward. And certainly in Xenophanes' time, as in most periods, Greek society was not prone to give lofty prizes to philosophers.

It is not surprising, then, that other philosophers, such as Socrates (in Plato) and the sophistic teacher-orator, Isocrates, later repeated Xenophanes' complaint. At Socrates' trial for "corrupting the youth" and religious impiety the 501 jurors (too many to bribe) convict him by a vote of 281 to 220. The trial then enters its penalty phase. Under Athenian law the prosecution proposes a penalty, and the convicted defendant makes a counter-proposal. Each of the jurors was compelled to choose one or the other. They could not consider any compromise. The prosecution proposes the death penalty. Socrates makes a glib, amazingly arrogant counter-proposal:

> There is nothing [no penalty] more fitting for such a man [as I] than free board at public expense. It's much *more fitting than* if some one of you *wins . . . at the Olympics*. Because that person just makes you *seem* blessed, but I cause you to *be* blessed; besides, the athlete does not need the support, but I do. (Plato, *Apology* 36E)

With these words, Socrates suggests that his penalty be free meals given at public expense, just like the reward the city gives to athletic victors. He justifies his position, as did Xenophanes, on the grounds that he does more good for the citizens than the athletes do. This proposal is so arrogant that it was predictable that eighty of the jurors who voted for his acquittal now voted for the death penalty.

Isocrates, a noted Athenian speechwriter, political commentator, and highly successful professor, was roughly Plato's contemporary. He too took his cue from Xenophanes' classic depreciation of athletic value: "I am astonished at how many cities decide that those who succeed in athletic competitions deserve greater rewards than those who, through mental exertion, come up with something useful."

Elsewhere, Isocrates elaborates on this complaint:

> The strangest thing of all is this: while people admit that the mind/ soul [*psyche*] is more important than the body, they still approve of those who compete in athletics more than they do of those engaged in the pursuit of knowledge [philosophers]. And yet it is wholly illogical to glorify those who engage in a lesser activity more than those who practice something more important.

And in yet another place, he complains that athletes "receive sizable rewards," while men such as he "get no respect" (*Epistula* 8.5; *Antidosis* 250; *Panagyricus* 1.1).

Isocrates' words "wholly illogical" clearly parallel Xenophanes' "it just is not fair." Both men consider themselves valuable intellectuals, highly beneficial to society; but they seem baffled and embittered by what they see as society's badly misplaced priorities. Of more importance, however, is Isocrates' innovation in terminology. As the converse of "body" [*soma*], he substitutes the word *psyche* for Pindar's "mind" (*nous*) and Xenophanes' "wisdom" (*sophia*). The word *psyche* in later texts is usually translated as "soul"; but often in Isocrates and Plato, classicists render it as "mind." For it is clearly intended as the seat of intelligence and all things mental as opposed to physical. The change from *nous*, "mind," to *psyche*, "mind" *or* "soul," in the traditional doublet of body and mind had a profound influence on Christianity's view of athletics, perhaps even on the demise of the Greek athletic festival. Near the end of this chapter we will look at what resulted when Christianity took over from the philosophers and other critics of athletes their depreciation of the body and physical excellence.

Isocrates accepts, even seems to recommend, the conventional Greek education of the young, whereby a child receives training in both physical exercise and academic subjects, such as literature and philosophy. But, contrary to the uses to which such passages are often put, he is not talking about Brundage's "well rounded" Greek culture or any "marriage of fine arts and sport." Rather, Isocrates is merely recognizing physical training for the young as part of a broad program of education, what he here and Greeks generally called *paideia*. It is called "General Education" in the American school system. It has nothing to do with athletes or their diversity. In fact, in the very same passage, Isocrates insists that the body (*soma*) is by nature "inferior" to the mind (*psyche*), and must be "subservient" to it (*Antidosis* 181–2). It is that last idea, subservience of the body to the soul (*psyche*), which will develop into Christianity's "mortification of the flesh."

Plato, too, called the mind the "mind/soul," *psyche*, and recommended moderate gymnastics as part of a program of general education or *paideia*. His remarks have nothing to do with Olympic athletes or with athletics of any kind. Yet sometimes they are misappropriated to support the idea of the Olympic athlete's diversity. Olympic historians have usually failed to distinguish Greek competitive athletics from Greek physical education of schoolboys. In the passage which they cite most frequently, Plato says the following: Exclusive attention to physical training may make a man "brutish, like an animal"; but exclusive attention to the mind may make him "brittle and soft." The body and mind should be cultivated together (*Republic* 3.410–12). The context unquestionably concerns the public education of the masses, not Olympic quality athletes. Perhaps the opponents of athletics during the Roman Empire also misappropriated the same passage. Whereas Pindar almost beatified some athletes, some critics bestialized athletes in the first and second centuries AD (see below).

Aristotle takes the major step that eventually even led to the utter rejection of athletics and bodily excellence in antiquity. Perhaps taking a wrong cue from Plato's remarks, Aristotle is the first to make physical and intellectual training veritable enemies of one another. In *his* education system, students will never be allowed to pursue physical education and academic subjects in the same year:

> The intellect and the body should not be subject to severe exertion simultaneously, as the two kinds of exertion naturally produce contrary effects, that of the *body* [*soma*] being an *impediment* to the intellect [*dianoia*] and that of the intellect, an impediment to the body. (*Politics* 1339a–b)

This passage is crucial. Aristotle's strange notion that exercise of the body and that of the mind are *antithetical* to one another caught on with later authors and it led to a total degradation of athletes in later literature. There were some earlier precedents on which these later authors could draw, as well. Isocrates asserted the body should be subservient to the mind. He and other philosophers, perhaps even out of jealousy, bitterly complained about the rewards which society heaped on the athletes. Yet no one had yet asserted that athletes, as a group, were stupid. The path lay open after Aristotle's thesis that physical training is detrimental to the intellect.

Hatred of the Flesh

In one of his lectures the first century AD author Dio Chrysostom represents the Classical philosopher Diogenes mocking the mental abilities of athletes: "these useless men ought to be cut up and served at a banquet . . . I really believe that athletes have less intelligence than swine." Elsewhere, he belittles a victor in the Olympic 200 meters, and issues a taunt, suggesting he is a coward: "A hare or a deer" could outrun you, and they are "the most cowardly animals" (*Oration* 7.11; 8.14). And Galen, a second century AD medical doctor, trying to dissuade young men from becoming athletes, wrote:

> All natural blessings are either mental or physical. Athletes have never even dreamed of anything mental. They are so lacking in reasoning that they don't even know if they have a brain. They cannot think logically at all – they are as mindless as dumb animals.

He too ends up comparing athletes to swine (*Exhortation to Medicine* 10–12).

Whether athletes had changed so that the athletes of Galen's Roman Empire were dumber than those of Pindar's time, we shall never know. There is no reliable evidence that athletes were *ever* noted for their intellects, even in Archaic and Classical times. Yet it is very clear that the literary commonplace remarks had changed.

The literary themes concerning athletes, body, and mind, had changed drastically. Where Dio sees the ability to run fast as the mark of a coward, the same ability is one of the most distinctive characteristics of Homer's epic hero, Achilles. And two of Achilles' most frequent epithets mean "fast of foot." To compare athletes to swine, as Dio Chrysostom and Galen do, contrasts sharply with the statement in *Odyssey* 8: "There is no greater glory for a man than what he wins with his hands and feet in the games." And it is likewise far from Pindar's comparisons of great athletic feats with the deeds of the gods. But Pindar lived in the days when *all* deeds of excellence – "of body *or* of mind" – were treasured; before the *body* had fallen, in literature, at least, to the onslaught of the *mind*, now often called the *psyche* and confused with the concept of the soul.

Naturally, Christianity pounced on these later authors' tirades against the body, and could link athletics right along with sex as a bodily activity antithetical to the soul. For the soul, *psyche*, in Christianity wholly replaced the concept of mind (*nous*) with Aristotle's notion that to cultivate the body is detrimental to its counterpart, now the soul.

The results can be seen not only in mediaeval man's abandoning athletic competition altogether, but also in his ever-increasing "hatred of the flesh." St. Paul, after disparaging athletes in a metaphor, boasts: "I maltreat my body and enslave it" (1 Corinthians 9.27). On an early Christian tombstone, the deceased author makes a similar boast: "On behalf of Christ, I abused my body with a lot of pain" (*Greek Anthology* 8.159). One can even detect the long arms of the Greek philosophers and the late Roman critics of athletics in the lives of some extreme ascetics. Dryethelm was a seventh-century monk who spent most of his life, even his old age, immersed in a river up to his chest, even in the freezing winters of notoriously cold Scotland. The Venerable Bede explains Dryethelm's purpose, namely: "his strong desire to punish his body. Out of a desire for heavenly benefits he subjugated his aged body" (5.12).

In the latter part of the nineteenth century, the movement called Muscular Christianity breached Christianity's anti-athletic bias. Its advocates declared that bodily exercise and athletic competition were acceptable, so long as they were "dedicated to the glory of

God." Thus the youth of the English upper classes decided to pursue athletics, but, technically at least, only as an activity subservient to purity of soul and religious piety.

Pierre de Coubertin brilliantly identified Christianity's morbid "hatred of the flesh" as the ultimate source of all the anti-athleticism he saw still lingering into the twentieth century (1986, 2.92 [1895]). It surrounded him even in the early athletic circles in which he moved, whose members were all devotees of amateurism. The partisans of the amateur movement warned everyone against the "excessive prominence given to bodily excellence and athletic success" (Gardiner 1910: 4). They insisted that there were "more important things than athletics" (Harris 1967: 114); that athletics should never be ranked among "serious" pursuits (Mahaffy 1879: 62).

Proponents of the amateur code also held that a proper athlete would never practice more than an hour or two a day, and never use a coach. All this was necessary for the subservience of the body to the mind. And in 1910 E. N. Gardiner could still write (as if just closing his Aristotle) about the "rival claims of body and of mind" (vii). As the movie *Chariots of Fire* vividly records, even at the 1924 Olympics Muscular Christianity and the anti-athletic strain of amateurism still held sway. Not only was Eric Liddell unable to run on Sunday; but also the British sprinter Abrahams had to hide his coach in a hotel; for to use a personal coach was even then to place too much importance on bodily excellence.

Mens sana in corpore sano had been the motto of British amateur athletics from their very start. It is now clear that it was never the ancient Greek Olympic ideal. Since those who adhered to this type of athletic ideal found nothing in Greek literature about ancient Olympic athletes cultivating their intellects, they had to look elsewhere for something to shore up their difficult position. They found something, but quoted only part of the sentence, and wholly out of its context. They found it in Fielding's popular *History of Tom Jones* (book 12, ch. 4).

Fielding himself probably used the original; for he quotes the full sentence: *orandum est ut sit mens sana in corpore sano*: "One should pray for a sound mind in a sound body." The sentence comes from Juvenal, a first century AD Roman writer of satires (10.356). Juvenal's subject matter in that passage has absolutely nothing to do with

Olympics or even athletics; the topic is, in fact, prayers to the gods. What is it, Juvenal asks, that we, all humans, should pray for? His answer is general good health, "a sound mind in a sound body." That's all the passage is about, "pray not to get sick, and not to go crazy." That's all. The phrase has nothing to do with any context in which people nowadays cite it wholly out of context. Least of all does it concern athletes of Olympic class. And it is, after all, rather commonplace. That is why Coubertin, after first endorsing this motto, eventually rejected it as being far too bland. He recommended that *mens sana* be replaced by a stronger version; namely, *Mens fervida in corpore lacertoso* (1986, 1.603 [1911]). His phrase literally translates as "a fiery mind in a muscular body." That was surely the baron's ideal, but there was nothing remotely like it in ancient Olympian ideology. There was nothing at all about the mind. And the notion that such big bruisers as the ancient wrestler Milo were prototype Rhodes scholars is just another piece of baggage toted along by the Olympic myth of Greek amateur athletics. That myth, after a long and destructive trip which began from nowhere, has now finally returned to its source. Unfortunately, we must still sometimes deal with the left luggage which it deposited along the way.

Questions of Profit and Social Class

The Myth of Amateurism

The ancient Olympic Games were strictly amateur – and for many centuries, so long as they continued amateur. (Brundage n.d.: 23)

For most of their history the modern Olympics took place under amateur rules, a complex set of ever changing regulations that restricted Olympic eligibility. Competition was open only to those who, in theory at least, had never received – nor even sought – any profit at all from athletics. As in his statement above, Olympic officials such as IOC President Avery Brundage claimed that strict amateurism was required in order to match the amateurism of the ancient Olympics. If the modern games ever lost their amateur rules, they would lose their authenticity, as well. They would no longer be a legitimate offspring of their ancient namesake. Many famous Olympians, Jim Thorpe and Paavo Nurmi perhaps the most prominent, were exposed and banned for breaking amateur rules. Even indirect profit caused Olympic officials to terminate a star athlete's Olympic career. The skier Karl Schranz was banned for endorsing a brand of ski equipment for profit. The decathlete Bill Toomey, while reigning Olympic champion and world record holder, was barred from all future competition. He had endorsed a quite legal nutritional supplement. Less than two decades ago, two champion American hurdlers were banned from the Olympics for life, along with Brian Oldfield, former world record holder – who was still throwing the shot more than a foot beyond the *recognized* world record. All three men were banned because they had competed for a few hundred dollars in a professional track and field league which failed almost as soon as it began.

Yet just a few years later, by 1988, the IOC had deferred all questions of eligibility to the international federations, which soon abandoned the unrealistic amateur restrictions. At Seoul in 1988, between her star performances on the track, television commercials featured Jackie Joyner-Kersee endorsing products, the very act which cost Bill Toomey his career only three Olympiads before. And in 1992, the first American "Dream Team," the best professional basketball players in the world, were allowed to compete for Olympic Gold. And today, even track and field athletes openly compete for sizable cash prizes before their national Olympic trials.

It all happened very fast. Olympic amateurism disappeared with amazing speed, and suddenly became a forgotten relic of another age. As I write today, it was only twenty years ago that those three prominent American athletes were still banned for breaking amateur rules, and ancient Greece was still our model of amateurism. Yet in 2000, in a poll of a class of twenty-four honor students at my university, not one had ever heard the assertion that ancient Greek athletes were amateurs. Only two claimed to know what an amateur athlete was.

Until about twenty years ago, almost all books and comments on the Olympics asserted that amateurism was the rule in ancient Greek athletics. But as the modern games finally shed amateurism, so did the ancient Greeks, who had become amateurs in 1879, when John Mahaffy published the words, "The contests were amateur performances, and . . . for centuries the glory and pride of Greece" (Mahaffy 1879: 63). There seems now in the world of Classical studies full agreement that amateurism was never practiced in ancient Greek competitive athletics. "Amateur athlete" is one thing the Greeks did not even have a word for. Since "athlete" means competitor for a prize, the concept as well as the phrase amounts to a contradiction in ancient Greece.

Why then for so many years did scholars and Olympic officials alike attribute amateurism to Greece? A brief summary of my book on this topic follows.[1] All but a few of our sports began in England in the second half of the nineteenth century (see chapter 2).

Victorian English society was strongly based on differences of social class. The wealthy, propertied classes held a strong sway over the working class. They tended to regard themselves as "aristocrats" who could happily avoid physical labor, and they sought desperately to maintain their privileged position. As formal competitions in athletics began to spread in the 1860s, these upper classes invented the concept of amateurism, and the first rules, formed in the mid-1860s, were founded on a strict class distinction that had nothing to do with profit. Anyone who was a "mechanic, artisan, or laborer" was classed as a professional, ineligible to participate in the athletic meetings of the "Gentleman amateurs" which were springing up at the time.

To bar a large segment of competitors increased the "aristocrats" chances of winning. By the 1880s, however, pressure from the larger public forced a modification of the rules. Rules against any profit replaced the rule against the working class. The effect was nearly the same.

The "Glory that was Greece" had a special power over Victorian England, appearing as the previous high point in Western civilization. These men succeeded in legitimizing their elitist sport by citing a supposed precedent in ancient Greece. There, too, they claimed, only the upper social classes ("aristocrats" or "nobles") competed in athletics. Although all other evidence had to be ignored, the partisans of amateurism could cite the policy of the ancient Olympics to award only a symbolic crown, and no financial gain.

These Gentleman amateurs found some obliging Classical scholars willing to promote their claims; to twist the evidence and argue that, at least in the Archaic and Classical periods, all competitors were upper class and they all refused to accept any kind of profit for their prowess. But this was simply the "brief bloom" of true Greek amateurism, as one Classical scholar called it (Shorey 1895: 322). Soon, the theory goes, Greek athletics degenerated, the lower classes and professionals began somehow to enter the lists, and corrupted the system so that it lost its pristine amateur state. Greek athletics then survived for centuries in this state of degeneration. But the Greek evidence wholly resists this theory of degeneration, and the scholars who made these arguments were compelled to treat the evidence very anachronistically.

Social Class of Ancient Athletes

Victors in the equestrian events were inevitably of the upper economic class, because to own racing stables necessarily required great wealth. Many equestrian victors were among the most powerful kings and politicians in all of Classical Greek history, or their relatives or associates. Hieron, monarch of Syracuse, Sicily, was the richest and most powerful man in the whole Mediterranean in the 470s BC. He won three Olympic and three Pythian crowns between 476 and 468, victories celebrated by Pindar and other noted poets of the time. Some of his deputies won Nemean victories. Other important Sicilian monarchs, such as Theron of Akragas and Anaxilas of Rhegium, were Olympic equestrian victors. Somewhat later, the wealthy and notorious Athenian politician Alcibiades achieved a pinnacle of ostentation, submitting seven chariot entries and inviting the entire group at Olympia to a banquet.

All these men knew that all Greece always noted who won the most prestigious events, and that the Olympics were a great source for political propaganda. Other equestrian victors were the leading people of their communities. Yet even here not every victor was from the elite upper class. In 480 BC the people of Argos, "horse-loving Argos," as Homer calls it, pooled their resources and sent a community chariot entry to Olympia. And they won, breaking the aristocratic monopoly of this event. The Sicilian monarchs Theron and Hieron won the chariot races in 476 and 468, respectively, but the resourceful Argives sandwiched in between them another community victory in 472.

For the great majority of ancient Olympians in the athletic events, in contrast, we have no evidence at all of their social standing, high or low. Although modern historians seem obsessed with knowing the social status of the victors, and somehow always find an aristocratic monopoly, ancient writers do not seem so interested in the question as modern scholars do.[2]

Of the victors in athletic events, fewer than a handful have a source to indicate that they were aristocrats or of the upper class before they competed. A seemingly certain case is the Athenian Kallias, son of Didymios, Olympic *pancration* victor in 472, *periodonikes*, and many times crowned at the Nemean and Isthmian Games. He was a political opponent of Pericles, and therefore was probably ostracized. People subject to ostracism were generally from the upper orders. But this Kallias seems not to be from the blueblood family of the Alkmaionids, probably the wealthiest and most prominent clan in Athenian history. The Alkmaionid Olympic victors named Kallias won equestrian, not athletic events.

A half-dozen or so athletes were certainly politically active, and some very rich. But it is impossible to tell whether or not they have their high material or political standing mainly because of their birth or because of their athletic success. Timasitheos of Delphi won the *pancration* in the late sixth century BC. He was executed for being a partisan of Isagoras, briefly Cleisthenes' co-archon and opponent at the end of the sixth century. But his involvement was in Athenian politics, not those of his own city, and far from proof of noble birth (Herodotus 5.72; Pausanias 6.8.6). The pentathlon champion Phayllos of Croton (see chapter 9) was so wealthy that in 480 BC he supplied his own warship for the battle of Salamis. Several athletes could afford a Pindar or Simonides to write their victory ode, and a prominent artist to fashion their statue.

One of Alexander the Great's lieutenants appointed Chairon of Pellene as sole ruler of his native city. Chairon, four times Olympic wrestling victor in the latter fourth century BC, found ruling more difficult than wrestling. His subjects detested his autocratic rule. The Olympic champion pentathlete Gorgos of Messene was part of an embassy sent to the Macedonian king in 232 BC. All these athletes have been cited as instances of the aristocracy participating in athletics, but most of them probably gained their wealth and prominence after their athletic career – and because of it. There is no source for any of these men which explicitly states that he is by birth aristocratic. There is no mention at all of their family's station in life.

On the other hand, there *are* some sources which explicitly attribute a non-aristocratic or even working-class origin to some athletes. Probably such success for a truly lower-class athlete was so rare that it attracted attention. But a rags to riches tale always appeals to most people, and that is probably why these victors' origins are mentioned. Our sources assign to the very first Olympic victor, Koroibos of Elis in 776 BC, the rather unaristocratic profession, "cook."

In 596 BC the victor in the boys' 200 meters, Polymestor of Miletus, was, we are told, a goatherd who practiced by running down rabbits. Herdsmen are near the bottom of the Greek social scale, and goatherd is the lowliest of the herding professions. Cowherds were ranked only slightly better, but a cowherd named Melesias from Barca, North Africa, won the wrestling at Olympia in 460 BC. He supposedly practiced by wrestling a bull. Not long before him, sources state that the farmboy Glaukos of Karystos won the boxing crown in 520 BC and was victorious in all of the Big Four. It seems that his father could not afford a hired man, since Glaukos worked the plow. But after his victories, Glaukos could afford to commission Simonides to write an epinician.

I think each of these stories of humble origins is suspicious. They have a general air of myth. Even if it is improbable that every one of them is wholly imaginary, one or all might be so exaggerated as to be of little worth in resolving the question. Yet at least there are some ancient sources *claiming* that these people came from a lowly background, and the theory of an aristocratic monopoly has no comparable set of sources. Further, these tales prove that Greeks themselves did not find humble birth impossible for an athlete, even if it seemed unlikely. So Aristotle cites the case of an Olympic victor, probably fifth century BC, who not long before his success at Olympia had been a fishmonger. Aristotle indeed cites his case as unusual, but expresses no doubt at all but that it is historically accurate. I therefore conclude that we should not either.

The Reality of Athletes' Earnings

Evidence for value-prizes, as I noted in chapter 1, starts with Homer, who refers to them not just in his mythological passages, but in his contemporary similes, as well. And Hesiod won a valuable tripod even in a musical contest. The Olympic officials' policy to offer no value-prize is certainly no proof of amateurism. In Herodotus some Greek prisoners of war tell the Persians that the only prize in the Olympics is the olive crown, and thus fool their captors into thinking that they are fighting a people which values honor only, never material gain (8.26). Unfortunately, these Greek prisoners have fooled some modern writers, too, who cite the passage as proof of Greek amateurism.

Anticipating a recent innovation in the modern Olympics, early sixth century BC Athens awarded 500 drachmas to any of its citizens who won at Olympia; an Isthmian victory paid 100 drachmas. Calculations of modern equivalents are of course imprecise, but it seems that it would take a skilled worker almost fifteen years to earn the amount which an athlete got for one Olympic victory. By the principle explained below in the section on the Panathenaic prizes, I must equate those 500 drachmas with at least $700,000 today, and probably closer to a million dollars or even more. An annual income of 500 drachmas thrust an Athenian immediately into the very wealthiest classification in Solon's timocracy (Young 1984: 129).

Other cities, it seems, granted a lump sum prize. An inscription from sixth century BC Sybaris indicates that an athlete named Kleombrotos dedicated a tenth of his Olympic prize to Athena, perhaps to make her a small shrine. Since a tenth of an olive crown would be impossible here, scholars believe that he refers to a large lump sum with which his city rewarded him. There are also reports, perhaps not so reliable, that this same south Italian city, Sybaris, along with its neighbor, the athletic power Croton, offered large cash prizes to lure athletes away from the Olympics.

There were scores of local or minor festivals in the Archaic period, and most offered value-prizes, some small, some large. Their worth varied greatly with the importance of the competition. Homer mentions a sacrificial animal as a prize. In the modest games at Pellene, victors won a warm leather coat. Tripods and bowls of costly metals were the prizes in festivals such as those at Tegea, Thebes, Marathon, and Sicyon. Others almost certainly offered cash prizes, especially after 500 BC. By the Hellenistic-Roman period, a purse of 6,000 drachmas was not uncommon. These festivals were literally designated as "money games."

We have already studied the poem of Xenophanes which deplores the great financial and other rewards which athletes receive. Here I merely note that the poem is wholly decisive as contemporary evidence, as early as the sixth century BC, of significant material gain. From the state, Xenophanes says, the Olympic victor obtains free meals and a gift, which would be a "treasure" to him, besides. The word for "treasure" here ordinarily is used for extremely valuable items, such as a gold ingot or a large quantity of highly valuable linen.

The most detailed information on prizes comes from a remarkable Attic inscription dating from the mid-fourth century BC. It contains a nearly complete record of the prizes awarded at the Panathenaic Games of that time, musical as well as athletic. These Athenian games were unusual in awarding second place as well as first.

The prizes in the athletic events at Athens were large amphoras of olive oil, the special product of the region. These amphoras were splendidly painted, with an athletic scene of the relevant event on one side, the figure of Athena on the other. Besides the value of the large amount of olive oil in these amphoras, each vase was a valuable work of art as well. Since the amount of oil in a prize was more than any athlete could use, the victors did not ordinarily keep the oil, but sold it to an olive oil dealer, who in turn exported to various markets. Therefore many of these amphoras have been found and are featured exhibits in museums around the world. They are large and held approximately 10 gallons or 40 liters of oil.

It is possible to calculate the value of the oil in each amphora. The dollar amounts I give here are extremely conservative, for the awards seem high as it is, and obviously it is better to err on the lower side of reality than to risk any exaggeration of the amount of the prizes.[3]

EVENT AND PLACE	NO OF JARS	EQUIVALENT IN YEARS' WORK	IN DOLLARS
200 meters			
Men			
First	100	2.82	135,600
Second	20	.56	27,120
Youths			
First	60	1.69	81,360
Second	12	.34	16,272

Boys

First	50	1.41	67,800
Second	10	.28	13,580

Pentathlon

Men

First	60	1.69	81,360
Second	12	.34	16,272

Youths

First	40	1.13	54,240
Second	8	.23	10,840

Boys

First	30	.85	40,680
Second	6	.17	8,160

Prizes for wrestling and boxing were the same as for the pentathlon; for the *pancration* they were more, first place being worth $108,480. Yet the prizes for athletes were the smallest in the three types of events on the program. First place in the chariot race earned a prize of 140 jars of oil, or 7.9 years' work, and $189,840. And before we accuse the Greeks of misplaced priorities in so much emphasis on athletes and horses, we must note that the music prizes, paid in gold and silver, not olive oil, were even bigger. The winner of the contest for *kithara* singers, something like our "singing guitarists" or even rock musicians, won a prize worth 3.53 years' work or $169,500. And whereas athletic events did not award more than two places, the singing-guitarist category had five places. And even a fifth rate musician received more ($33,900) than any second rate athlete ($27,120 in the 200 meters, $16,272 for a boxer).

At the end of Plato's *Republic* Socrates tells a tale of a man named Er, who died on the battlefield but returned to life to tell people of the wondrous events which he witnessed in the afterlife. This Myth of Er, as it is known, contains an extended account of ideas usually associated with the mystery religions and reincarnation. This is not the place even to summarize the long and complex events and topography which Er relates. I focus only on that part relevant to our immediate subject. The souls of people who have just died are judged by their conduct in their previous lives, and long-term rewards and punishments allotted accordingly.

When the souls are ready to be reborn and return to earth, some are allowed to choose their next life. The choice comes to Atalanta, the tomboy of Greek mythology. To us she is best known perhaps by the tale where she challenges all suitors to a foot race, where their prize for victory is her hand in marriage, but losers are put to death. But even in other, earlier myths she excelled at physical activities ordinarily done only by men and even in actual athletic competition. About 580–540 BC an early and influential poem called "The Games of Pelias" generated a number of vase paintings of the topic. In several, Atalanta is in a formal wrestling contest – attendant judges and all. In the Myth of Er when her opportunity to choose a life presents itself, "seeing the immense rewards and honors of the athlete," she chooses to be an athlete in her next time on earth. So the proposition that an athlete receives great honor and a lot of money is assumed from the outset. Perhaps Aristophanes sums it all up in his play titled *Wealth*: "To have contests in music and athletics is the thing most suitable to Wealth" (1162–3).

9

The Athletes

Tales of the West

The ancient Greeks had their superstars, just as we do. The most proverbial of all ancient athletes was Milo, a wrestler from the Italian city of Croton. Legend had it that he could stand on a greased discus, and no one could move him off; also that he could snap a headband just by expanding the muscles in his temples. Milo is the one who reportedly began to lift a newborn calf every day until he could hold a full-grown bull over his head. In the rest of the story he supposedly carried the bull aloft into the stadium, butchered it, and devoured the whole thing – chasing it down with 6 gallons of wine. He met his end, according to the myth, when his hand was caught in the cleft of a split tree, and wolves came along to eat him.

The amazing thing about Milo is that his actual achievements are as impressive as his fabulous ones. He won in at least six Olympiads in a row, probably seven. The evidence is slightly confused, because his first victory in 540 was in the boys' category; yet the adult victories make him reigning Olympic champion for at least twenty years. The inscription on the base of his statue at Olympia read: "This is the handsome statue of the handsome Milo, who won seven times at Olympia – without ever touching his knee to the ground" (Simonides No. 25 Page [No. 153 Diehl]). He was finally dethroned in 512 BC by Timasitheos – a fellow citizen of Croton.

When he retired he was six times *periodonikes*, Winner of the Circuit (see chapter 2), competing in only the one event, wrestling. Besides his six (or seven) Olympic victories, his record was: six Pythians, ten Isthmians, and nine Nemeans. His total of at least thirty-two victories in the Big Four capped a career that was wholly unparalleled (Harris 1967: 111).

Croton is the most notable athletic program known for its success. Croton, a colony founded rather early on the sole of the Italian boot, enjoyed its first Olympic victory when Glaukias won the 200 meters in 588 BC. From that date to 548 BC, Croton's sprinters won the 200 more than half the time, six times in eleven. In one Olympic 200 final six of the first seven finishers were Crotoniates. Then there was a long gap in their 200 victories, until 508 BC, when Ischomachos of Croton won the first of his two victories. It is probably relevant that in that gap fell the entire career of Milo. It is tempting to suspect that the government temporarily switched its resource support from the runners to the wrestling program during that gap. As soon as Milo was finally beaten, the sprinters resumed in a remarkable string of victories, losing only once from 508 to 480 BC. And even in 480 BC the victor was a former Crotoniate champion, Astylos, who had changed his allegiance to Syracuse, Sicily, "to gratify Hieron, the Syracusan monarch" (see chapter 3). Historians naturally conclude that Astylos himself was gratified by a large sum of money.

Astylos' victory in 484 BC was the last ever won by Croton, whose regularly recurring name suddenly disappears altogether from the victory lists. The city never won another Olympic crown. I, at least, am compelled to believe that some sudden change in Croton's political or fiscal being terminated a program that had long recruited athletes from other cities and supported them well. It recruited outstanding individuals in other professions, such as art. And it was the home of one of the best medical schools in the whole ancient world, which trained Democedes, the most successful athletic director of antiquity. After he left Croton, Democedes had a meteoric and highly unusual career, capitalizing on his earlier medical training.

The political climate of Croton was far from ordinary. For decades in the period in question it was the home of the brilliant and eccentric mathematician, mystic, and politician, Pythagoras, whose circle generally controlled the government. Pythagorean politics, like everything else about this giant of a man, are left rather confused and baffling in our sources. He himself never published a word. But it probably is not mere chance that so successful an athletic program took place in the context of Pythagoreanism and Crotoniate medicine. A mathematician such as Pythagoras might well have come up with a special program of biomechanics or muscle conditioning. A dietitian, as well, he, or a Democedes, with a special interest in diet, could have discovered an exceptional training table (or even performance-enhancing drugs?).

One other athlete from Croton deserves mention here, the pentathlete Phayllos. Although he never won an Olympic victory – an omission ancient sources explicitly note – many prominent ancient authors stress his excellence for a variety of reasons, as do almost countless later writers (Gardiner 1910: 209–10). In a play of Aristophanes (*Acharnians* 214–16), Phayllos is the first athlete who comes to the mind of a man wanting to name the exemplar of a fast runner.

Phayllos' only known athletic achievements are a 200 meter victory at Delphi and two pentathlon crowns there, probably all before 482 BC. Yet Pausanias specifically states that he is the most noteworthy of all the athletes with statues at Delphi, and begins his description of the precinct of Pythian Apollo with Phayllos. Alexander the Great supposedly honored his memory. Herodotus and others relate his activity during the Persian War, when he commanded his own private warship, manned by his fellow citizens, at the crucial battle of Salamis (Herodotus 8.47). So much is probably all true and impressive. Yet what modern scholars know him for best, a long jump of over 50 feet, is almost certainly pure fiction (see chapter 3 and appendix B).

Besides Croton, other cities of Magna Graecia – the civilization of the Greek colonies in Sicily and southern Italy – produced numerous Olympic victors, especially in the athletic golden age of the sixth and fifth centuries BC. We have complete records, of course, only for the 200 meters. But of the 200 meter victories from 588 to 408 BC, thirty (65 percent) belong to these western Greek colonies. In contrast, in that same period, Athens never won in an athletic event at all, Sparta only twice.

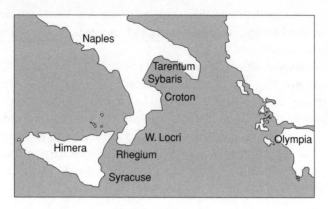

Figure 9.1 Magna Graecia about 500 BC

Several victorious pentathletes besides Phayllos came from Magna Graecia. Tarentum, not far from Croton in southern Italy, produced three pentathlon winners in the mid-fifth century BC. Ikkos, the first of these, was just as well known for his activities as a coach, and probably trained the other two Tarentines who won the pentathlon crown (see below). Other western Greek champions, such as Tisandros and Euthymos, were boxers or wrestlers.

Outright myths were told about Euthymos, from the city of western Locri, on the toe of the Italian boot. On his return from Olympia, he supposedly vanquished the ghost of one of Odysseus' sailors, who would annually demand the sacrifice of a young woman. Euthymos married the rescued maiden of the year, and later was honored with a hero cult. In a historic bout Euthymos was once the opponent of the remarkable Theogenes of Thasos (see chapter 4). And like his famous opponent (below), Euthymos may have later received outright hero worship (Harris 1967: 119).

Besides dominating the 200, western victors were common in the 400 meters and distance races as well. One of the more impressive distance runners was Ergoteles, who won an Olympic victory in 472 BC, apparently lost in 468 BC, but won again in 464 BC, competing for the western colony of Himera, Sicily. Born and no doubt trained in the distance running capital of antiquity, Crete, he switched to Himera perhaps in mid-career. He went there when, for unknown reasons, he apparently had to leave his native Knossos, Crete, as an exile. He was twice Victor of the Circuit, capturing two crowns in each of other contests of the Big Four. His statue was in the Olympic Walk of Fame, and the poet Pindar wrote an Olympic victory ode for him.

Distance runners rarely received as much admiration as the other ancient athletes – or as much attention from later authors. Some exceptions are the Argive runners Ladas and Ageos, along with Drumos of Epidaurus. These three athletes were all reported to have run non-stop after their Olympic victories to announce their success at their home cities in the eastern Peloponnesus, a distance (through mountains) hardly believable for a single run (see also appendix C, on the modern marathon).

Athletes and Heroes

After Milo, Theogenes of Thasos was the athlete most renowned. Although he had fewer Big Four victories than Milo, he had more total victories; namely, 1,300. Theogenes' commemorative inscription at Delphi proudly boasts of his achievements in both boxing and *pancration* (Ebert 1972: 37):[1]

> Thasos never produced anyone like you, son of Timoxenos, and of all the Greeks you deserve the most praise for strength. The same man was never before crowned at Olympia in both boxing and pancration. Of your three crowns at the Pythian Games, one was by forfeit. No mortal had ever achieved that before. Ten victories in nine Isthmiads; for the announcer twice declared you the first earthling to win the boxing and the pancration on the same day. You have nine Nemean victories, as well, Theogenes. The total of all your victories is 1,300. And never, I'll swear, in twenty-two years were you ever defeated in boxing.

For an athlete who specialized in the two most brutal events, the total of his victories is so amazing that a few classicists even doubt its honesty. It is not, however, impossible, since he competed in many local events around Greece. Thasos is an island in the very northern Aegean, so his record implies that he was on the athletic circuit abroad for a large portion of his life. He was a Winner of the Circuit, but only two of his many victories were at Olympia. Yet those two crowns set a record (see chapter 4) and spawned some tall tales.

Family pride and loyalty were especially strong elements in Greek society, and the world of athletics was no exception. In a poem for the victorious son of a champion sprinter, Pindar wrote: "Blessed and to be celebrated by poets is the Olympic victor who lives to see his son duly crowned in the Games" (*Pythian* 10.22–6). Many fathers today vicariously share their sons' athletic careers and might find the sentiment especially apt. Yet this beatitude applies more fully to the boxer Diagoras of Rhodes than to any other. He was a Victor of the Circuit. His only Olympic victory came in 464 BC, when he was clearly no longer a young man.

Diagoras' first two sons, Damagetos and Akousilaos, won Olympic victories in the adult category, boxing and *pancration*, just twelve and sixteen years, respectively, after their father's success. Then in 432 BC his third son, Dorieus, won the first of his three successive Olympic *pancration* crowns. In 404 BC two of Diagoras' grandsons, as well, won at Olympia, each the child of a different daughter. One of those daughters, probably Kallipateira, is the widow about whom later authors spun a tale of a woman who successfully violated the ban on women's presence at Olympia (see chapter 10).

Various stories were told about Diagoras and his descendants; some no doubt true, others no doubt false. The story most popular in antiquity is still popular today in Greece, part of a living heritage. It is told not only by such well-known Greek authors as Plutarch, but also by Cicero, whose Latin version gave it some life even in later Western European literature: "*Morere, Diagora; non enim in caelum ascensurus es*": "Die Diagoras; for you will not ascend to the heaven" (Cicero, *Tusculanae Disputationes*, 1.46.111). To us, this comment may seem pointless, if not tasteless. But in antiquity and in context, to tell someone to die is the highest compliment that may be given to a man. It is another occurrence of Pindar's *ne plus ultra theme* (see chapter 6), for it means that Diagoras has reached the summit of human achievement and happiness. There is nothing more for him to accomplish; the only thing left is to become a god, which no human can do.

In Greek religion, a "hero" is technically a distinguished human who has died. Not a god, he is more than human, and ordinarily receives sacrifices and prayers. Diagoras never reached the status of a hero, but a few athletes from the early years were later worshipped as heroes. They all seem to be fifth century BC or earlier. All evidence for their hero cults comes from texts many centuries after they lived; namely, in the time of the Roman Empire. The most certain case is Theogenes, the Thasian with 1,300 victories. Centuries after his death, the belief was that his father was not a human, but the god Herakles himself. The Thasians' supposed neglect of his memory caused a period of crop failure, until the oracle at Delphi told them that they must restore his honor. Thus an inscription dated about 500 years after his death proves that in the first century AD, at least, he possessed a hero shrine in his native island. Visitors to it, presumably making prayers for his help in things such as healing, were expected to pay a certain amount of money (Harris 1967: 118).

To judge from all the evidence, it is not likely that any athlete received hero worship in his own day or even a century or two later. A few other early victors achieved almost mythological status, and were honored centuries after their deaths with a cult and sacrifices. Pausanias says that in the second century AD citizens of Dime still sacrificed to their much earlier fellow citizen, Oibatas, who won the 200 meters in 746 BC, the sixth recorded victor. The legend attached to his cult generally follows a common pattern: the great athlete who gets no respect from his fellow citizens. In anger, he puts a curse on them, which later causes such difficulty that they must consult the oracle at Delphi. The oracle informs them that their troubles arise from their maltreatment of the athlete, whom they must now propitiate and worship with a hero cult in order to end their misfortune (Pausanias 7.17.14). A fifth century AD inscription probably copied from an earlier version confirms Pausanias' account.

The tale of the boxer Kleomedes displays a slight variation of this theme. Kleomedes won his event in 492 BC, but by dealing lethal blows to his opponent. The Olympic officials stripped him of his victory on the grounds that he had won unjustly. He probably did use illegal, hatchet-like blows to his opponent's mid-section (Brophy 1985: 178–82). Much angered by the judges' decision, Kleomedes went somewhat berserk and returned to his homeland, the remote

Aegean island of Astypaleia. Still in a fit of pique, he pulled down a pillar in the local school building. The roof came down, killing sixty schoolchildren. When pursued with stones by the irate citizens, he took refuge inside a chest located in the temple of Athena. When the Astypaleians pried the lid of the chest open, it was empty. Kleomedes was not in it. Bewildered, the people consulted the oracle at Delphi, whose response claimed that Kleomedes was "the last of the heroes, and no longer mortal." The response further instructed the people of Astypaleia to institute hero rites for the athlete. They did (Pausanias 6.9.6–7).

Yet another version of this theme of the neglected athlete whose reputation is upheld by the Delphic oracle concerns Orrhippos of Megara. The 200 meter victor of 720 BC, later reports say he was the first athlete to compete in the nude. In the version of the legend which the local priests told to Pausanias, Orrhippos' loincloth fell off in the middle of the contest. However, he did not stop and won the race. Others then imitated the practice of the victor (Pausanias 1.44.1). But if a runner's loincloth came off, one would think it would take him at least a moment to adjust to the mishap. And in a sprint, the loss of even a moment would seem to exclude victory. Later, the oracle at Delphi told the Megarans to erect a statue in honor of this athlete. The whole story sounds exactly like one of those etiological tales that always raises suspicion. The athletes' nudity has no need for an etiological explanation.

Nudity, Massage, and Coaches

Many moderns find it rather strange, or even shocking, that Greeks competed publicly in the nude. They repeatedly ask, "Why did they do that?" But our own Western culture is imbued with the Judeo-Christian tradition, wherein, from the very start, nudity itself is an intolerable, shameful state. The moment that Adam in the Garden of Eden realizes he is naked, he judges it wrong and shameful, and feels a need to cover himself (Genesis 3.7–8). Ancient Greeks had no comparable uneasiness toward nudity in their cultural background. In art, even their gods they usually portrayed nude. Greek men would not have allowed their wives or daughters to appear nude in public, because of the possible appearance of promiscuity. But nudity itself, especially male nudity, was no cause for shame.

If asked why they performed nude, I suspect that most ancient athletes would have responded with a simple, "Why not?" "Athlete" is a Greek word, but the word "athletic" is very rare in antiquity. It appears a handful of times after Aristotle, but what we call "athletics" Greeks regularly called "gymnastics," literally "things done nude." The word *gymnos means* "nude." A "gymnasium" is, etymologically, "a place to do things naked." There is also a practical reason why Greek athletes competed in the nude.

Massage occupied a very important place in Greek athletic training, and in preparation for competition. It is much harder to give a thorough massage to someone wearing clothes, even shorts, than someone who is nude. Massage also provides the answer to another question that moderns often ask: "Why did the ancient athletes apply olive oil to their bodies?" Scholars have unnecessarily offered a number of inventive answers, while overlooking two obvious reasons. First, Greek peasants who work outside today still show the effects of the hot, dry Greek summer. It parches the skin until it may look almost like leather. The olive oil, perhaps even having a very small value as a sunscreen, kept the athletes' skin from such unhealthy dryness.

Second, and no doubt just as important, was again the primary role of massage in Greek athletics. There are two words for an athletic coach in antiquity. Etymologically, both denote the coach's basic function as a masseur. One of them, *aleiptes*, means "one who applies oil"; the other, *paidotribes*, means "one who massages the young." Massage is employed in modern athletics, especially boxing; but there is nothing nowadays to match its importance in antiquity. Masseurs of all periods have used oil, of course, to make their pressurized movements on the body smoother, more effective and enjoyable.

For ordinary workouts, athletes may have applied the oil themselves, or to one another; the *aleiptes* would have performed the task for competition. After they were oiled, all athletes who were preparing for the wrestling or *pancration* dusted themselves with a fine powder so that they would not be so slippery as to impede the contest. So a victory by forfeit (British "walkover") was termed "without dust," as we might say "without suiting up." The term was sometimes then applied to any victory which was won without competition, even in other events. After their workout or competition, the athletes (and laymen, who did the same at their local *palaestra*) would scrape off the oil and dust with a flexible metal tool, a *strigil*, designed only for that very purpose. *Strigils* are characteristic of painted scenes in a *palaestra* or gym, and were sometimes buried with the deceased. Archaeologists have found a large number of them, which museums around Europe display in their cases. It is not certain whether athletes in the non-combat events, who indeed were well oiled, were also powdered. To judge from a poem by Bacchylides (10.19–26), a contemporary of Pindar, runners did not use powder.

The use of coaches goes far back in Olympic history, at least to the sixth century BC. Coaches naturally had many duties besides massage. They spent time helping an athlete improve his technique, and most devoted great attention to the athletes' diet. Philostratus complains about the finicky precision diets which coaches of the Roman Imperial period forced on their charges. In the Classical period and later, athletes were generally notorious for eating large quantities of meat. Pausanias claims that the first all-meat diet was invented by an early fifth century distance runner and *periodonikes*, Dromeus. Cheese was the staple of earlier athletes' daily fare (Pausanias 6.1.10). Surprisingly, other sources state that the all-meat diet was first developed in the sixth century BC by Pythagoras. Since the famous philosopher otherwise preached strict vegetarianism, the reference may be to another man by this name.

Partly because diet was regarded as so significant, there was a close relationship between athletic training and medicine. As the most famous athletes came from Croton, the best-known athletic trainer was Democedes of Croton. Educated as a medical doctor in Croton's noted medical school, Democedes' meteoric career probably surpasses that of a very successful American football coach. Some football coaches in America earn one or several million dollars a year. Aegina, an island especially proud of its athletes, offered Democedes an immense salary, far more than twelve times that of a skilled worker. But the good doctor signed only one-year contracts. The next year, Athens hired him away from Aegina by paying him almost double that.

After a year in Athens, he accepted a position with an even higher salary at the island of Samos, just off the coast of Asia Minor. But the Persian King Darius soon captured Samos, along with its wealthy "Director of Public Health." At first Darius held Democedes chained in prison. But learning of Democedes' medical skills, he induced him to cure the queen's abscessed breast and to reset his own royal ankle, which had become dislocated in a hunting accident. Democedes probably had experience treating such dislocations, since they were no doubt a common athletic injury. Overjoyed, Darius gave the doctor immense amounts of gold, a huge mansion, and dining rights at the royal dinner table – everything but the freedom to leave Persia to return to Greece. Later, the story continues, after he won permission, by a ruse, to leave temporarily, Democedes reached Croton. There he married the daughter of the illustrious athlete, Milo. He then foiled Darius' efforts to force him back to Persia, and presumably Democedes and his bride lived happily ever after (Herodotus 3.129–33).

Herodicus, too, was a medical doctor who practiced coaching and sports medicine. He might have been the mentor of Hippocrates, the most famous doctor of antiquity and author of the medical oath still in use today. Herodicus' training methods involved grueling exhaustion workouts and a very strict diet (Plato, *Republic* 3.406a). Ikkos of Tarentum, Italy, himself an Olympian and champion pentathlete, probably coached the other two Tarentine pentathlon victors who won in the early fifth century BC. He was one of the few who, like a very small number of modern professional athletes, believed in sexual abstinence for athletes in training (Plato, *Laws* 840a). Some modern coaches are famous for being the first coach to win so many national or conference championships, or career victories. Ancient coaches, too, could reach certain notable milestones. In his *Odes*, Pindar mentions several of his patrons' coaches by name. Melesias, who some (not all) ancients say was an Athenian, coached several of Pindar's Aeginetan victors. In *Olympian* 8 Pindar announces that the particular victory which he celebrates there marks the thirtieth in Melesias' career, presumably in the Big Four. Like Ikkos, Melesias was himself a former champion athlete.

10

Women and Greek Athletics

Women Competitors at Olympia

There were never any women's events or categories in the ancient Olympics. Several women Olympic victors, however, appear in the official lists. In the equestrian events the victory did not go to the jockey or charioteer. The winner was the owner of the victorious racing stable, who need not even be present at Olympia. No rule excluded equestrian entries owned by women.

The first and most notable of these women victors was Kyniska of Sparta, who won the four-horse chariot race in 396 BC. The fractured base of her bronze statue has been found at Olympia, with a portion of the dedicatory inscription. Fortunately, the full text was already preserved elsewhere:

> The kings of Sparta are my fathers and brothers. I, Kyniska, winning with my chariot and swift horses, have set up this statue. I declare that I am the only woman from all Greece to take this crown.

There was an ancient rumor that her brother Agesilaus had encouraged her to breed horses and enter, just to prove to some people that the equestrian events were won "not by excellence, but by money" (Plutarch, *Agesilaus* 20.1). This matter has fueled a vigorous modern debate between the more vocal advocates of women's rights, who tend to regard a woman Olympic victor as a heroine, and their detractors, who retort that the victory, from the start, was meaningless. Judging from related matters, I suspect that the story that would detract from her victory was either politically motivated or a bit of misogynist propaganda. For one thing, to view a chariot victory as paltry goes against the grain of the entire history of Greek festival competition, which made the chariot victory the most prestigious of all (see chapters 4 and 8).

A number of items suggest that Kyniska, her contemporaries, and most people thereafter took her victory very seriously and saw it as a genuine achievement. Her dedication of a statue, commissioned from a distinguished artist, along with the above inscription (which is datable by its style to her exact time), indicates that she herself was very proud of her victory. She could hardly have thought it a joke or a trick. And another, smaller statue of her chariot was placed inside the temple of Hera. She entered her chariot again in the next Olympiad, 392 BC, and won again. The Spartans erected yet another statue in her honor at Sparta. Later, they made a hero shrine for her there (Pausanias 3.15.1). It is virtually impossible to imagine that all that is founded on a meaningless sham.

It was not long, probably less than three decades after Kyniska's success, before Euryleonis, another Spartan woman, won an Olympic victory. This time it was in the two-horse chariot race; her statue, too, was enshrined at Sparta. These two Spartans were not the only women to gain Olympic victories. Bellistiche, a Macedonian woman, had become the girlfriend of Ptolemy II, Philadelphus, King of Egypt, when he was widowed. She won two Olympic crowns, the first in 268 BC in the four-horse chariots for colts, the second in 264 BC when her team won the two-horse chariot race for colts, the first time the latter event was ever held. About two centuries later, another woman, Theodota of Elis, won that same two-horse event. She came from a family with many and various equestrian victories at Olympia.

In the later centuries, at least, teenage girls[1] did compete every four years in a foot race at Olympia, not at the Olympic Games but at the Heraia. This festival, held in honor of Zeus' wife Hera, took place every four years, but separately from the Olympic Games and at a different time of the year. Our only source for these contests is Pausanias (5.16.2–4). A board of sixteen women administered the

Heraia, of which the main purpose, it seems, was to weave a new robe for the statue of the goddess. A similar cult practice took place elsewhere. At Athens, for example, at the Panathenaic festival for Athena, the weaving of a new robe for Athena every four years occupied a major place in the festival.

I paraphrase and summarize Pausanias' rather lengthy account: at the Heraia in Olympia the "Sixteen" sponsor foot races for teenage girls (*parthenoi*), divided into three age groups. The youngest run first, then the middle group, and last the oldest. They use the Olympic stadium track, shortened by one-sixth. They wear a kind of mini-dress open at the right shoulder so that it exposes that breast. The winners (presumably one from each age group) receive an olive crown (just as the Olympic victors) and also a portion of meat from the sacrifice to the goddess. They may also dedicate their portraits inside the temple of Hera. The reduction in the length of the course parallels the shorter women's tees on our golf courses.

Without himself expressing any opinion, Pausanias says that the Eleans told him that the Heraia was a very ancient festival, dating clear back to the mythological time of Pelops and Hippodameia, and began with his race for her hand. They also told Pausanias a second such aetiological myth as an alternate.

Most classical historians accept the Eleans' assertion that this race for teenage girls was a very ancient cult practice (Drees 1968: 29; Scanlon 2002: 115–16). But its antiquity is open to strong doubt (Harris 1967: 179–80). There are indeed several cogent reasons to suspect that the Heraia is a late addition to the Olympic festival calendar. Pausanias' second century AD report is our earliest and only reference. It seems unlikely that such a distinctive festival and race could pass for about a millennium wholly without any mention whatsoever in extant literature. Even Pausanias, at pains to make it clear that he is merely recording what he was told, seems unsure of its truth. Priests and tour guides are known to embellish, even to invent interesting details about their site, especially when they must resort to mythology, as here.

Pausanias' description of this race fits the gender customs in his own days of the Roman Empire (see below) better than Archaic or Classical Greece. Furthermore, his words never imply that the competitions are Panhellenic; or even that these are young women who come from other cities of Greece. It is more likely that the only competitors were drawn from the local population. All this makes for paltry evidence of anything comparable to our own women's Olympic participation, even at a late date, no matter how much many of us wish the case had been otherwise.

Women, Girls, and Sport in Greece

Since the general topic interests many readers, I review some of the more general evidence for women's physical training and competition in Greece. In its earliest years Sparta may not have been so "Spartan" as we know it from later historians; that is, there might not have been so strict a militaristic society and austere way of life. Poetry thrived early. A seventh century BC Spartan poet named Alcman had an excellent reputation among ancient Greeks, but nothing of his work survived the Middle Ages. About 150 years ago an ancient papyrus was found in Egypt with substantial parts of a poem which he composed for a chorus of teenage girls. That poem, along with some early figurines of young female runners found in Sparta – one of them very muscular – make it certain that the young women of Sparta competed, perhaps in teams, in some kind of intramural foot race, probably an annual event. The figurines wear a "gym suit" much like those worn at the Heraia as described by Pausanias.

Even when military training dominated Sparta, Spartan women married later than in other places, such as Athens, and they had more freedom. They did not live with their husbands. There was compulsory physical training for the teenage girls. The Greeks attributed the establishment of this compulsory physical training to Lycurgus, the Spartan lawgiver, who said that strong mothers produce strong babies who, in turn, become strong soldiers. Lycurgus figured strongly in the tale about how the Olympic Games originated in an agreement which he and Iphitos made (see chapter 2). Although Lycurgus himself is almost certainly legendary, there is no doubt but that Spartan girls went through the rigorous training attributed to him. The fullest account is in Plutarch (*Lycurgus* 14.2–

15.1). He says that the teenage girls' physical exercise in Sparta went beyond foot races, that it also included throwing the javelin and discus, and even wrestling. Like the young men, the contestants performed nude, Plutarch says, and did their "parades in the nude," while the young men watched.

"The nudity," Plutarch insists, "was in no way shameful, because modesty prevailed, and not intemperance." Yet he goes on to say that these "nude processions, disrobings, and contests [*agones*] in full view of the young men" had the intended effect: it affected them "erotically" and instilled in the young men a "desire for marriage." Lycurgus made bachelorism a dishonor. Others, such as the Athenians, found these nude activities and athletic contests rather licentious and downright titillating. In a play of Euripides' a character chides Menelaus for having so loose a wife as Helen. But what does one expect of a girl from Sparta, he asks, where the young women run around half-dressed or naked with the young men, and "share the race-courses and wrestling buildings with them?" (Euripides, *Andromache* 595–602).

Girls or young women did not contend in wrestling or pentathlon events outside of Sparta. It is possible that Athenian girls, mostly but not always pre-pubescent, had an annual foot race at Brauron (on the coast not far northeast of Athens). The race would be part of a festival in honor of Artemis called the Arkteia, or "Bear Celebration." But the evidence for this race is far from decisive, and this is no place to examine the complex scholarly disputes on this subject. In the vase paintings in question, the girls are not nude.

There is no reliable evidence for any international or large-scale athletic competition for females of any age in materials that could date such competition to the BC period. I therefore tentatively conclude that there probably was none. Yet a truly remarkable inscription from the first century AD raises some important questions, while it answers some, as well. On a statue base for his three daughters a proud father tells of their achievements. The inscription was found at Delphi a long time ago, but much of the text is illegible and still in dispute. I give a translation which omits all the possibly tendentious or conjectural restorations which have been offered for the illegible parts (Dittenberger 802; Miller 1991: 103):

Herrmesianax, son of Dionysios, citizen of Caesarea Tralles and [illegible] [dedicates to Pythian Apollo these statues of] his daughters, citizens of those same [illegible]. Tryphosa, winner of the 200 meters at the Pythian Games when the Directors were Antigonos and Kleomachidas, and at the following Isthmian Games, when Juventius Proclus was Director; she was the first of the young women to do that. And for Hedea who won the chariot race in armor at the Isthmia, Cornelius Pulcher, Director. She won the 200 meters at Nemea under Antigonos' directorship, and at Sicyon, when Menoitios was Director. She also won at the Sebasteian Games at Athens in the lyre singing for the young when Nouios was Director . . . [illegible]. And Dionysia, who won the 200 meters at [illegible] . . . and at the Asklepian Games at sacred Epidauros, when Nikoteles was Director.

Not only do we here have evidence for teenage girls or young women competing internationally, but also at three of the Big Four festivals except the Olympics. Naturally, historians speculate about the categories of competition. Was there a division exclusively for girls, or did these young women compete in the boys' division, and triumph over the boys? It seems very likely, at least for some period of time, that a female division separate from the boys was instituted at these games. Significantly, there is no evidence of any counterpart at the Olympics.

Of great significance is Tryphosa's record, first young woman to win the Pythian and Isthmian 200 meters, back to back. This record not only suggests competitions separate from the boys but also proves that the teenage girls' competitions were a recent innovation. Otherwise, so simple a combination could not be a record. The men's records by this time were extremely complex, for in the course of many centuries, almost every conceivable combination had been achieved (see chapter 3). Even the boys' records by this time would have been many times more complex than Tryphosa's. Therefore the inscription itself establishes that such competitions for girls could not have gone back for centuries. Once more all evidence suggests that there were no international contests for girls or young women until the Roman Empire. Whether they continued long after the mid-first century AD period or were short lived we will never know, unless a similar but later witness comes to light.

Apart from Pausanias' account of the Heraia at Olympia, I can find no other evidence of even local competitions for girls. There is, however, yet one more fascinating item, which dates from near the end of antiquity. A fourth century AD Roman mosaic from Sicily depicts several young women in very skimpy dress, just a bra and small panties. It is therefore known as the "Bikini girl mosaic." Some are playing ball, but others are performing events of the Greek pentathlon: running, long jumping, and throwing the discus.

Because of their dress, some scholars conclude that the bikini girls are not athletes, but merely entertainers, probably performers at a men's gathering. But Lee's (1984) close comparison of these scenes with vase paintings of athletes doing the same events confirms that they are indeed executing the same movements as male athletes. He concludes that the girls are not entertainers, but athletes in competition. We need not, however, choose between these two interpretations, entertainers or athletes. Athletics themselves at this time are becoming little more than entertainment. It is a period of known decline at Olympia, and the other festivals have disappeared by the fourth century AD. A program for the chariot races in fifth century AD Byzantium demonstrates how far those days were from the golden age of Greek athletics. The program lists not only the races, but also the intermission entertainment offered between races. In between one pair of races, the entertainment is provided by tightrope walkers. Another interlude features actors and clowns. And yet another states that during the intermission there will be an exhibition of "ancient Greek athletic contests" (Oxyrhynchus Papyri 2707; Harris 1972: 242).

Women as Spectators

Few modern works on the Olympics omit mention of the law which banned the presence of women at Olympia during the festival; for it is probably the most sensational matter reported in antiquity. Women who violated the ban were punished by death: thrown off a cliff called the Typaean Mountain – or so Pausanias states (5.6.7). Flocks of modern authors eagerly stress the seemingly gruesome detail, as if at the foot of the cliff there lay a pile of skeletons. But we tend to attribute to this ban against women *far* more importance than it deserves. First of all, we know it never happened, not even once. No woman was ever pushed off this mountain. Again, the only source is Pausanias, and he himself asserts that *the law was never invoked*. He knew of only one violation, and in that case the woman, Kallipateira, was a daughter of the famous Rhodian Olympic champion, Diagoras. Her three brothers, all Olympic victors, possessed a total of six crowns among them. And her son, Peisirodos, had just won his own Olympic victory (see chapter 9). Because she was a widow, she had brought him to Olympia herself so that he could carry on the illustrious family tradition. She came disguised as a man, as Peisirodos' coach, in fact. In her elation at his victory she jumped the fence of the coaches' enclosure and – or so Pausanias' story goes – thus exposed her whole body to view. The officials then saw that Peisirodos' coach was really a woman, but out of respect for her family, "instead of penalizing her [Pausanias does not use the verb "killing"], the Olympic officials let her go entirely unpunished" (Pausanias 5.6.7).

Elsewhere, the text of Pausanias asserts: "They [the Olympic officials] do not prevent unmarried women [*parthenoi*] from watching [the games]" (6.20.9). Some therefore think that a distinction was drawn between married women and unmarried women, the former barred from Olympia during the games (5.6.7), the latter admitted as spectators (6.20.9). Others think that this sentence of Pausanias contradicts his earlier passage about the ban on women, and that there is a corruption in the text. So Harris (1967: 183) writes: "It is certainly one of the many corrupt passages in the text of that author." I agree that both passages could not be authentic. I regard the statement about unmarried women, *parthenoi*, as a corrupt misstatement mostly because it enters the text *wholly* out of context, and even interrupts it. Its only context is an explanation about the priestess of Demeter.

The passage (with no omissions) reads: "There is a special seat from which the priestess of Demeter watches the games. They do not prevent unmarried women [*parthenoi*] from watching. At the end of the stadium where the runners start is a grave of Endymion." The sentence in question is an obvious *non sequitur*. In context, the sentence about *unmarried* women's freedom to watch appears to be an explanation why the priestess of Demeter is allowed to watch; but it comes wholly "out of the blue," because the priestess of Demeter *was married.*

Throughout Greek religion, sacerdotal personnel for *married* female divinities, such as Demeter, were regularly themselves married, while unmarried priestesses served virgin goddesses, such as Athena (Turner 1988: 926). I suspect that a very late scribe (probably a Christian), who was copying Pausanias' text, thought he had resolved a contradiction, by inserting the sentence about unmarried women. He seems not to have known that the most renowned priestess of Demeter was, in fact, Regilla, the wealthy Roman wife of Herodes Atticus, Pausanias' contemporary. The special seat was perhaps first made specifically for her, since she and her husband were the greatest benefactors of Olympia in the second century AD (see chapter 12).

A parallel question as to whether or not women were in the audience of Greek tragedies is still not fully settled. So I think we are still unsure whether or not any women, married or not, were allowed to attend the Olympics. A passage in Pindar implies that women of both categories were spectators at the games in Cyrene (or perhaps even the Pythian Games); but that passage is at least susceptible to another interpretation (*Pythian* 9.98–100). Once more I stress, however, that the question was probably not so important as we make it. In Classical Greece, it is not likely that many women, married or unmarried, even sought to attend. And even if permitted, I doubt that they attended, unless they were local inhabitants. Few husbands or fathers would have invited them to come along on the trip to Olympia.

11

Between the Greek and Roman Worlds

Years of Turmoil

After Olympia lost the role as center for Panhellenic peace efforts, which it had briefly enjoyed in its "Golden Decade" of the 470s BC, Greece entered more than a century of political chaos and military devastation (see chapter 5). The period of 470 to 350 BC or so coincides generally with what we call the Classical period and even the "Golden Age of Greece." We regard that time so highly because, in the main, most of the well-known dramatists, philosophers, orators, and statesmen fall into that period. And many of the artists of note date from then as well; as do the most impressive structures, such as the several buildings on the Acropolis, especially the Parthenon, and those in the Agora (marketplace) below it. It is probably not fortuitous that almost all of these illustrious people and things are Athenian.

The Athenians of the Classical period, with an uncanny sense of history, engaged in these pursuits so brilliantly as to emerge as the jewels of Greek civilization in the eyes of humankind in future centuries. Thucydides (1.10.2) even foretells that his generation of Athenians will occupy a special, probably even exaggerated place in world history. It was indeed an Athenian golden age in some ways, but in other ways this period was the nadir of Greek civilization. During the Peloponnesian War the inhumanity with which the Greeks treated one another is downright shocking. War was a way of life. Both Athens and Sparta sought to be the only dominant power in the Greek world, which was compelled to suffer with them.

There were so many battles even before the official outbreak of the Peloponnesian War that the two principals signed a "Peace for Thirty Years" in 446 BC. It had a shaky life of about a decade before the main and devastating Peloponnesian War was officially declared in 431 BC – perhaps just as Pheidias made the finishing touches to his Zeus at Olympia. Throughout the war, the games continued, Olympiad for Olympiad, attracting citizens from all parts of a strongly divided Greece. There seems no indication that contestants or spectators acted in ways that reflected the deep hostilities among the Greek states. Yet war booty was still offered and dedicated to the god, as before and after the war.

Virtually all Peloponnesian states were active allies of Sparta, and in 428 BC they convened at Olympia. Otherwise, Elis and Olympia played no special role in the war. Yet the Eleans offended their Spartan allies by barring them from the Olympiad of 420 BC on the grounds of an incident so complex that its details would serve no purpose here. In long-delayed retaliation, shortly after the official end of the war in 404 BC, Sparta invaded Elis. Elis lost the war, much capital, and its power over the Alpheus valley; but it was allowed to retain control of Olympia itself and the games.

Elis was only once forced out of its role as host of the Olympic Games, and only once did an army invade the Olympic sanctuary as the games were actually taking place. Those invading soldiers were the Eleans themselves. Elis and its allies had long been having battles and skirmishes with Elis' traditional foe, the Arcadians, who occupied the vast, mountainous territory to the east. In 364 BC the Arcadians successfully invaded Elis and occupied Olympia by military force. When it became time to hold the games, the Arcadians, not the traditional hosts, the Eleans, sponsored them.

The wrestling final of the pentathlon was in progress when the Elean army arrived, there to fight for the territory it claimed as its own. The two armies engaged in battle right then and there, even reaching the very heart of the sanctuary, the Altis. The battle was heated and long, lasting on into the night. Arcadians and their allies occupied the roofs of the buildings, including the great temple of Zeus, and attacked the Eleans with missiles that rained down from above. Eventually, the Eleans were driven back out of the sanctuary, which the Arcadians immediately fortified against further attacks. The games were finished and the Arcadians remained in control (Xenophon, *Hellenica* 7.4.29).

Before the next Olympiad, however, a multinational truce gave Olympia back to Elis. The Eleans hosted the 360 BC games as usual, writing off those Arcadian Olympics of 364 BC as a "Non-Olympiad." The rest of Greece, however, the record book, and history all recognized it as legitimate and it "counts."

When the Eleans invaded the sanctuary they seemingly broke the Olympic truce, which they themselves traditionally announced throughout the land. A ban against invasion was perhaps the major feature of the Olympic truce. Of course, the Eleans did not regard their own actions as a violation, since they viewed the occupiers of Olympia then as imposters. The truce itself is widely misunderstood in the modern world, and the IOC has been the major misinterpreter. Despite many statements to the contrary, the Olympic truce was never a time when all the Greek nations ceased all wars and military hostilities. They often continued to wage war against one another throughout the actual time of the games – as a reading of Thucydides' *History of the Peloponnesian War* will make almost painfully clear.

All classicists who have studied the evidence agree on what the truce really was. It forbade invasions of Olympia itself. Most importantly, it prohibited anyone from stopping anyone, athlete or spectator, on the way to or from Olympia and the games, even if required to pass through a hostile country to make the trip (Lämmer 1983: 47–70). Thus, by ancient standards, the USA and the USSR, when they compelled their own athletes, willy-nilly, to boycott the 1980 and 1984 Olympics, respectively, would have committed classic violations of the ancient Olympic truce.

We know of only one case where the truce was actually invoked, and then it seems to be the city of Athens rather than the Eleans who declared the violation. In 360 BC, when the Eleans had resumed sponsorship, some soldiers of Philip II, king of Macedon and father of Alexander the Great, detained an Athenian named Phrynon. He was on his way to the Olympics when they robbed him of all he had. A violation of the truce was declared. Phrynon asked the Athenians to appoint him as an ambassador, so he could go to Philip and ask for his stolen possessions back. Philip received him in a friendly way, gave him back his belongings and more, and then apologized, saying that his soldiers did not know it was the "Holy Month" (Miller 1991: 69).

The Kings of Macedonia Start a New Phase of Buildings

King Philip II was himself an Olympic victor in the equestrian category in 356 and perhaps 352 and 348 BC. His son Alexander would not deign to compete even in the Olympics, reportedly asserting that he should compete only against other kings. Alexander and his father left a large imprint on the site of Olympia. Philip had grand plans to take over all of Greece. The orator Demosthenes perceived these intentions and warned the Athenians about Philip's threat. Yet he could not stop the power-hungry Macedonian, whose annexation of Greek territory proceeded quickly until he gained mastery of Greece in 338 BC.

Knowing Olympia's Panhellenic appeal and eminent status, Philip began an opulent monument to himself and his royal family, a round building well inside the Altis, just west of the temple of Hera. He was assassinated in 336 BC. His son Alexander, later nicknamed "the Great," soon acquired the throne and responsibility for finishing the family shrine at Olympia, the round building thereafter called the Philippeion. It was a shrine. It was the only structure inside the Altis dedicated to a human, and was carefully designed to suggest that the royal family was perhaps more than human, perhaps more like the deities who possessed the temples nearby. Like the temple of Zeus, it had a roof made of marble. Like the gods' temples, it had an inner *cella* extravagantly finished with the finest materials. Around that *cella* stood statues of the Macedonian family, fashioned in gold and ivory – like Pheidias' Zeus. Everything was designed to give the impression of divinity (Drees 1968: 122). The Philippeion at Olympia must have given a head start to Alexander's campaign to convince everyone that he himself was actually a god, a project which succeeded in the rest of the world, if not in Greece. In a little more than a decade, he was master not

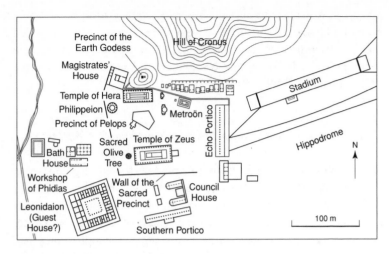

Figure 11.1 Site of Olympia, about 325 BC

only of all Greece, but virtually the entire ancient world known to Mediterranean peoples. In the east, his army advanced all the way into India.

Other important buildings were erected about the same time as the Philippeion. For centuries, all pilgrims to Olympia were compelled to find whatever accommodation they could. Even the wealthy usually pitched a tent. About 325 BC, Leonidas, probably from the island of Naxos, personally financed the construction of a huge guesthouse. There, VIPs, at least, could find agreeable lodging more like that to which they were accustomed. Called the Leonideon, the building was nearly square and very large, about 260 feet long and 240 feet wide, much larger even than the temple of Zeus. A series of rooms, much like hotel rooms, surrounded a plush central courtyard. The Leonideon had both an inner and an outer colonnade, so that guests could walk around with a view either of the sanctuary or of the courtyard.

Another important structure was erected in this same period of increased building. The Painted Colonnade, better known as the Echo Colonnade, was an independently standing portico about 270 feet long. It ran along almost the entire eastern boundary of the Altis, stopping not far from the Treasuries along the north, leaving just a passageway to the stadium to the east. The colonnade also served to separate the sanctuary proper from the athletic site and the games, which may well have become increasingly secular.

Later, athletic facilities were added to the west of the sanctuary, as well. The *palaestra* (see chapter 4) at Olympia dates from the next century, and was built between the Altis and the Cladeus River. Here wrestlers and pancratiasts would train before the games. For the boxers, one room would have held punching bags, which are illustrated in the vase paintings. By the third century BC, large sections of most *palaestrae* were being used for academic, rather than athletic, development. Rooms for young students and lecture halls for philosophers and orators eventually predominated over the space devoted to athletics in *palaestrae*. But I find it hard to believe that most of the *palaestra* at Olympia was, from the start, intended for academic use. I know of no evidence that would suggest boys or very young men lived nearby in sufficient numbers to fill a school there. Elis had its own *palaestra*. Even rather academic *palaestrae* retained dressing rooms, a room where athletes put oil on their bodies, washrooms, and baths.

The baths at Olympia were exceptional. Some went back to the fifth century BC, the oldest in Greece. They were small structures located just south of where the *palaestra* was built later. Filled by fountains, they were just deep enough to cover the athletes' hips. The only large outdoor swimming pool known in Greece was in Olympia, and also built in the fifth century BC. It was almost 80 feet by over 50 feet, and more than 5 feet deep. Even before the *palaestra* was built, some of the smaller baths were heated. Some new baths were now built to replace some of the earlier ones, and in the Roman period many Roman-style baths were added.

The gymnasium was built after the *palaestra*, and is the natural completion of the Greek building program on the site. In antiquity, a gymnasium was not an enclosed building, like ours, but an open practice track, that in Olympia actually longer than the stadium. There was always a *palaestra* wherever there was a gymnasium, and the latter became a generic term for the combination of the two. Olympia apparently had no covered practice track, not even a narrow one like that in the lower site at Delphi. The one long track

at Olympia was surrounded by colonnades on all sides, with some
rooms for the athletes on the west side.

The Program of the Later Period

There is surprisingly little evidence about the procedure of actually
producing an Olympiad. Most that is known with any certainty
comes from Pausanias' account in the second century AD. Evidence
dating earlier is seldom consistent, nor is it precise enough to make
the important questions clear. Much of the account which appears
below follows a format suggested by Lee (2001: 71–4)

Heralds left Olympia to announce the coming Olympiad and
proclaim the truce, probably a couple of months before the games.
Before the large crowds and vendors came, athletes arrived for whatever verification or selection process there may have been. In the
later years, they reported to Elis first rather than directly to Olympia,
and even trained there (see chapter 5).

On the first day of the festival, the athletes, close family members, and coaches, took the oath in the *Bouleuterion* or Council
House, in front of a statue of Zeus the Oath Enforcer. They swore
on the entrails of a sacrificed boar that they would do nothing to
harm the games, especially that they would not cheat. The judges
likewise swore that they would be impartial and fair. There followed a formal validation of the athletes' qualifications and selection. Since these matters were already determined, this rite was
ceremonial only, probably a reminiscence of a real feature of the
very early years. After they were added to the program in 396 BC,
the contests for heralds and trumpeters were also held that first day.

The schedule of an Olympiad, after it was extended in 468 BC,
apparently reserved the second day for the equestrian events and
the pentathlon. The focal point of it all, the Great Sacrifice to Zeus,
probably took place in the morning of that third day. A solemn
procession left the altar of Hestia, Goddess of the Hearth. It
included the judges, the priests, ambassadors representing a number
of states, the athletes, and the others who had attended the ceremony of the oath. With considerable pomp, the procession made
its way to the altar of Zeus. There the priests sacrificed a number

of oxen. It was called the Sacrifice of One Hundred Oxen, but in reality it is not likely that so many were used.

The priests butchered the victims and carried the thigh pieces to the top of the altar to burn them in honor of the god. By Pausanias' time, the altar was about 20 feet high, for the ashes from the burned bones were not removed, but allowed to build up. The meat from the victims, as in all Greek sacrifices, was served to the participants.

Probably shortly after 200 BC, when the program of the boys' contest had reached its full size, the afternoon was given over to the boys' contests, which earlier must have occurred along with the equivalent men's competitions. In the evening, the heroic rites and sacrifices were held at the hero shrine of Pelops. All remaining contests, the foot races and combat events, fell on the fourth day. The hosts sponsored a banquet for all the participants in the evening. The officials probably held no separate prize-giving ceremony, but awarded each victor there on the spot when he won. Before they were awarded as the prizes, the olive crowns rested on a special ornate table made by an artist named Kolotes (Pausanias 5.20.2; Gardiner 1910: 121; Lee 2001: 71–4).

The Great Sacrifice to Zeus during the Olympic festival itself, once in four years, was of course not the only time when the priests sacrificed to Olympian Zeus at his altar. There were monthly sacrifices there, and to many other gods at their individual altars. These included several distinct special aspects of Zeus, such as Zeus the Purifier and Zeus of the Thunderbolt. By Pausanias' time in the second century AD, there were a great many altars of various kinds for various gods around the site, and the priests performed at least fifty monthly sacrifices at them in a carefully determined order. It is not surprising that so many cults to lesser deities were eventually established at Olympia. The same thing to some degree had happened almost everywhere by this time. Athens, too, seems to have been almost cluttered with altars of gods and shrines for hero cults. Furthermore, we recall, Olympia was the most Panhellenic of all Greek sanctuaries; it would have attracted new altars for gods worshipped around the Greek world. With its famous statue of Zeus and its aura of a powerful tradition, the site had always excited an extraordinary awe in those who visited it. To the Greeks, Olympia was an especially holy place.

The Later Centuries of Olympia

Rome takes the Prize

Alexander had expanded his father's empire almost beyond imagination (see chapter 11). When he died in 323 BC, some of his father's closest aides and some of his own fought one another for control of the vast conquered territory. After decades of war among these "Successors," three men emerged victorious and still alive. They agreed to form three main kingdoms, one for each to rule. Antigonos Gonatas received Macedonia, that is, Greece. His was an uneasy rule, with internal and border wars almost constant, but the sanctity of Olympia was respected and protected, except for a brief and insignificant incident. The Olympiads marched on as always.

A number of the third century BC victors were from Macedonia or near there. But another new trend began. Even more athletes from the grand new capital of Egypt, Alexandria, named after its founder, won the Olympic crown. Their success grew until they dominated the list of victors. Many victors still came from mainland Greece, but in the latter half of the third century BC many athletes from Asia Minor, or the islands off its coast, such as Cos and Rhodes, won as well. The competitors from Egypt and Asia were all Greeks, who had their own cities, usually not far inland. If a few who came from Asia were not actually Greek, they were Greek speaking and lived in a wholly Hellenized city that was part of Greek civilization.

Always stable and highly respected by all, the Olympics under-
went their biggest change when the Romans took over Greece in
146 BC. Some other Greek cities had fallen to the invading Romans
before the soldiers of the general Mummius captured Corinth,
the hub city of all mainland Greece. It surrendered readily, but the
Roman Senate ordered Mummius to sack it anyway. Somewhat
reluctantly, he razed it and burned it to the ground. Partly in
atonement, he then made offerings to Greek sanctuaries. He was
especially fond of Olympia. He dedicated a statue of Zeus there and
twenty-one oversized golden shields, which were permanently affixed
above the colonnade at the main eastern entrance to his temple.

Rome was not an especially tyrannical overlord. So long as a
conquered people paid their taxes and submitted to the power of
Rome, recognizing it as their supreme sovereign, the Romans tended
to let their subjects keep local customs, language, and religion.
Augustus, *de facto* first emperor of Rome by 27 BC, strengthened
that policy of tolerance.

Greek athletics continued because of this leniency toward local
customs. Roman rule, however, was not kind to Greece or to
Olympia, both of which declined noticeably throughout the pre-
Augustan era of Roman control. Yet enough Roman dignitaries
erected their statues at Olympia during that period to prove that
there was no open friction between the Olympic officials and their
overlords. Only one Roman committed a violent act against Olympia. In 86 BC the Roman general Sulla, who needed to finance a
foreign war, robbed Olympia and other Greek sanctuaries of their
treasures. Somewhat later the sanctuaries were indemnified and there
was no real permanent damage.

Even before Sulla, the Romans had entered a long period so
marred by the devastation of civil wars and internecine strife that
they concentrated on their problems at home, paying less attention
to their subject provinces. Olympia and its games suffered more
from neglect than from any malevolence. And all Greece had apparently entered a kind of financial depression. There is a paucity of
victor statues in the Altis in this period. And all the Olympic equestrian victors came from nearby Elis, a clear indication that no one
could afford racing stables, or at least not the transport of their
horses and gear to the games.

Just before Augustus attained his position of full power, his friend Marcus Agrippa had helped restore the damaged temple of Zeus. There were other signs that the site and games might be redeemed under Augustus' imperial rule. In 12 BC the emperor induced King Herod of Judea to subsidize the Olympic festival. No Roman *ever* entered an athletic event at Olympia, but the few exceptions to the Elean monopoly of the equestrian events are also the only Romans known to sign up at all. In the early years of Augustus' control, a few people closely linked to him, even the future emperor Tiberius, won equestrian events. Probably no Roman Olympic victor ever set foot on Olympic soil.

Augustus judged it expedient for his administration of Greece if Greek athletics and Olympia should prosper. He formally reorganized the Circuit, and in 27 BC had added a fifth festival to the Big Four, the Actian Games. The astute ruler wished to glorify Actium, on the northwestern coast of Greece, because that was where he had so decisively defeated Antony and Cleopatra and thus become sole master of the entire empire that Rome controlled, including Egypt. The Actian Games were "isolympic"; that is, they followed exactly the same rules as the Olympics. He instituted other isolympic games in Greece and Italy, one of the most prestigious of which was in Naples. All contestants were Greek.

The new emperor eventually declared himself a god, and at Olympia he founded a cult to himself. He dedicated his own statue there, three times life size. But it did not look much like him, because it was made in the likeness of Zeus, replete with thunderbolts (Drees 1968: 119). The stadium was renovated at his command – almost as it is now – and he subsidized Greek athletics in general. The Eleans allowed subsequent "divine" emperors to place their statues within the Altis. If they wished the games to continue and even to improve, they had no choice. They were compelled to go along with these excesses, which were often committed as much on behalf of successful policy as megalomania.

The next three emperors neglected Olympia somewhat, but the most notorious events in all Olympic history took place thereafter under Nero, who was the quintessence of megalomania. A fan of the chariot races in Rome, he wanted to win the chariot race at all festivals of the Greek Circuit in a single year. So he ordered the Big

Four to hold their festivals all in the same year, 67 AD. Olympiad 211, scheduled for 65 AD, was therefore postponed for two years.

Badly deceived by flattery and delusion, Nero also fancied himself a great singing musician. So he made sure that contests in music, tragedy, and singing were added to festivals that lacked them, such as the Olympics. His singing was appallingly bad, but no judge dared award the crown to anyone else. In the chariot race, he fell off his chariot, but claimed the victory anyway. He was assassinated within a year, so the Olympic judges, who now had to repay the bribes which he had given them, declared the Neronian Olympiad a non-Olympiad which did not count. But the Olympiad number 211 was kept, lest the chain be broken, and just two years later came Olympiad 212.

A Brief Renaissance

When the Olympics recovered in the latter first century AD from the depths which they had reached a century earlier, they were no longer the same institution as before. The ancient world, especially the Greek world, was not the same. No longer a conglomerate of individual city-states, it was almost a single world, with generally common religions, government, and culture. Large urban centers had replaced many of the scattered villages and smaller cities of former days.

In the first half of the second century AD, the Philhellenic Antonine emperors, Hadrian and Antoninus Pius, strongly supported Olympia. The Olympics once again became a grand institution which attracted large numbers of spectators and athletes. An athlete's prestige, if he won, was once again enormous, and it now spread throughout the broad Roman Empire. The Olympic Games entered a new and successful phase, which can aptly be called a "renaissance" (Scanlon 2002: 53–4). It lasted for most of the second century. Philosophers, orators, artists, religious proselytizers, singers, and all kinds of performers went to the festival of Zeus. Most of them attracted large crowds as they spoke or exhibited whatever they brought.

The principal construction projects at Olympia in the first century AD consisted of a large villa built just for Nero's only visit, and a clubhouse for the athletes' union. The union had already become an important force by then, and negotiated directly with the emperor's office about such things as government awards, pensions, and festival regulations. Archaeologists uncovered the union house only recently. Begun during Nero's reign and completed later, it was located in the southernmost part of the Altis. In 1994 the excavators found in it a bronze plaque with a surprising inscription. It proves that genuine international Olympics survived even longer than was thought.

One of most important features of Olympia's architecture was built in the mid-second century AD, its construction no doubt triggered by the renewed success of the games during this renaissance. For about a millennium, all who came to the Olympics had suffered from thirst in the blazing August sun. Archaeologists found temporary wells among the earliest remains, but there was never adequate water. And now the Roman-style baths around the south part of the Altis exacerbated the problem. A very wealthy Greek, Herodes Atticus, and his very wealthy Roman wife, Regilla, funded an elaborate fountain which was both a practical solution and a work of art. Water, piped in from a tributary of the Alpheus, entered into a large semi-circular basin. Emerging from 83 gargoyle fountains, it was then channeled all around the site. Behind the basin rose a semi-circular colonnade more than 100 feet high, with a series of niches built into its upper level.

Statues of the three Antonine emperors – Hadrian, Antoninus Pius, and Marcus Aurelius – were erected on the roof. Within the niches below were placed statues of Herodes, his wife, and his family, along with some of the imperial family. Zeus himself seems to have occupied the middle niche. A large marble cow, inscribed as "a gift from Regilla," stood atop and center of the wall which separated the basin proper from the system of fountains. Perhaps her generosity influenced the Eleans when they chose her as the priestess of Demeter.

Olympia's Sun Finally Sets

The prosperity of the Olympics in the second century AD seems to have faded badly in the course of the next. Not only does Africanus' victory list end with the Olympiad of 217, but also subsequent ancient authors no longer seem to care enough about the games to mention any new Olympic victors in any extant text. Evidence for the few later Olympic victors of whom we know comes not from literature but from excavated inscriptions written in antiquity.

Formerly, the last certain and precisely datable victory was (probably) in 241 AD, when Publius Asclepiades of Corinth won the pentathlon. For centuries and even a decade ago, historians thought that the very last known Olympic victor probably was not a Greek, but an Armenian prince named Varazdates. Varazdates' supposed victory is attested only in a murky Armenian source (Moses of Khoren, *History of Armenia* 3.40).[1] Since Varazdates reigned from 374–8, conjectures place his rather doubtful victory, mentioned only in an Armenian history of Armenia, in the 360s AD. But the bronze plaque found in 1994 at the athletes' clubhouse not only gives us new names, it also reveals that truly international Greek Olympic Games continued at least until 385 AD, much longer than any previous evidence suggested.

The plaque contains the names of the victors in the combative events who come from both the mainland and Asia Minor. The list extends from the first century AD almost to the end of the fourth. The last two entries are for two brothers from Athens, Eukarpides and Zopyros, who won boys' events in 381 and 385 AD, respectively (Ebert 1995). It is perhaps somewhat reassuring to learn that the last known victor is from Athens rather than Armenia.

There is no doubt, however, but that the very institution of the Olympic Games slowly and continuously declined throughout the third and fourth centuries AD. It was then interrupted by a journey into obscurity which lasted a millennium and a half before the games could resume their glorious course. In 267 AD barbarians called the Heruli had overrun the major cities of Greece, and a defensive wall built around the central Altis about the same time suggests that they attacked Olympia as well. A little later an earthquake damaged all the buildings. They were soon repaired, but for the next century, repeated flooding from both nearby rivers caused further damage. Although they had long been foundering, the games themselves had somehow endured until at least 385.

Earlier in that same century, the emperor Constantine the Great had made Christianity the favored religion throughout the Roman

Figure 12.1 Remains of the temple of Zeus, victim of repeated earthquakes; photo by author

Empire. He had moved its capital to that ancient and magnificent city which has probably enjoyed and suffered more historical highs and lows than any other in the world. To Greeks, it had always been named Byzans, later Latinized to Byzantium. Constantine called it New Rome, but it was far better known as Constantinople, named after him. It is now Istanbul.

From there in 391 AD Theodosius I, a Christian and the emperor of the Roman Empire, banned all pagan worship and issued an edict that all pagan temples be closed. It was probably then that someone stole Pheidias' priceless statue of Zeus. It was last seen still in place at Olympia in 384, but it was known to be in Constantinople by 395. There in the new capital, the story goes, after a few decades gracing the palace grounds of a rich man named Lausus, the Seventh Wonder of the Ancient World burned to the ground along with Lausus' mansion. Whatever the case, it disappeared without a trace known to survive today.

Zeus' temple and his Olympic Games may well have lasted beyond the 391 edict and into the fifth century. Respectable evidence would date the actual termination of the cult of Olympian Zeus not to the reign of Theodosius I, but to that of his son, Theodosius II, who in about 426 reinforced his father's ban on all remnants of paganism. This time the Olympic priests and officials complied. By then barbarians had taken over most of Greece anyway, and soon Christians took over Olympia. They converted the workshop of Pheidias into a church for the celebration of the Mass.

The Christian village, however, never became large. What had been Olympia was no longer a hospitable place. Major earthquakes, floods, and more barbarians continued to frustrate the inhabitants. By 620 even the Christians had abandoned the site. Many feet of alluvial sand buried it for many centuries before archaeologists began to uncover its ancient treasures. Never again were there Olympic Games in antiquity. Yet we have Olympic Games now.

Ancient Greece had scores of other athletic festivals, some truly important. But the games at Olympia were the ultimate in athletic competition. Pindar, we may recall, compares the way they eclipse the others to the way the sun outshines all other stars in the noon-day sky. The Olympic Games were in a class of their own. Above all, for most of the centuries that they were held, the Olympics were a showcase for human physical excellence, where mortals, as Pindar said, could "resemble the gods." Of equal importance, the Olympics played so unique a role in antiquity that they passed beyond the athletic events proper to exemplify, even to symbolize, all of ancient Greek civilization at its best. That, in fact, is precisely the reason why they were revived in modern times.

13

The Origin and Authenticity of the Modern Olympic Games

The Ghosts of Olympics Past

It was Plato who first suggested that the Olympics be revived in modern times – or rather it was his ghost. The ghost of Plato expresses this "odd idea" in an 1833 poem by the Greek poet Panagiotis Soutsos. The phrase "odd idea" comes from a reporter with the British Broadcasting Corporation (Mark Whitaker, radio interview with author, 2000). He claims we are so accustomed to the modern Olympics now that we fail to notice how odd, innovative, and unique an idea it was to revive the ancient games. It is true. Many features of our culture have probably evolved, in part, from similar features in ancient Greece; one thinks of such things as drama, democracy, and even modern medicine. Others, such as some types of art, imitate Greek prototypes. Yet it seems that we have *revived* no other Greek institution. It *is* an odd idea, or so it seems when one reflects on it.

People often deplore the modern Olympics for their corruption or supposed inferiority when compared to their ancient counterpart – rather unfairly, I believe. In essence, the two are the same. The modern Olympics, too, represent the pinnacle of excellence and prestige, and in most significant ways they are not much different from the ancient version. The principal difference, I think, is how much the modern Olympics dwarf their ancient ancestor in size. At Sydney 2000, more than 10,000 athletes from 200 countries

Figure 13.1   Panagiotis Soutsos

competed in 300 events. That's big. In the heyday of the ancient Olympics, for example, the fifth century BC, there was a total of 14 events and perhaps up to 300 or so competitors. In antiquity, perhaps as many as 40,000 spectators could watch the games. Because of modern electronic communication, the whole world watches today's Olympics, which have become the greatest show on earth. Almost anywhere on earth one can view them on television, and almost everywhere on earth people *do* view them.

The games' return to Greece in 2004 is a mark not only of a respite from their century-long odyssey, but also a return to their roots – not only their ancient roots but to their *modern* roots as well. Most people who care still think that the modern games are the brainchild of a Frenchman. Baron Pierre de Coubertin, and Coubertin alone, Olympic officials and the media have told us for a century, was the first and only person to have this happy idea. Then he almost single-handedly implemented it, holding the first modern

Olympics in Athens, in 1896. To this day the IOC and the media still maintain this illusion, and most people, even most Greeks, follow it like a flock of sheep. But it is quite wrong.

Our modern games are, in fact, the brainchild of a *Greek*, and *modern Greece* had Olympic Games before Coubertin was even born. England had Olympic Games when Coubertin was still a toddler. Coubertin *was* important to the revival, and deserves much of the credit. But so do some other unsung fathers of the Olympic idea, an idea which I believe Coubertin never could have conceived on his own. It is difficult to believe that an institution so massive and esteemed as the Olympics could have had so humble a birth. After faltering baby steps, the Olympic revival movement suffered an extended, troubled youth, for decades barely surviving while on the verge of dying from neglect. Having come full circle, robust, and nourished again on their native Greek soil, the modern games will have reached full maturity as they march on to China, which was a different world from Greece in the 1830s – but is now just a large part of a single human civilization.

Our Olympic Games are not so much a revival of the ancient Greek games as a genuine continuation of them. The modern Olympics are not Olympics in name only. Despite great differences, they have the same spirit, the same dedication to the pursuit of excellence, and the same goal of bringing out the best in people. And most importantly, there is a legitimate, direct Greek line of descent which can be traced all the way from the simple ancient stadium over in Olympia, through Sydney and all the rest, on up to the modern Olympic stadium at Kephissia in Athens.

The seed of the modern Olympic revival was first planted on Attic soil by a modern Greek poet, but it was a seed which that poet, Panagiotis Soutsos, took from the ancient olive at Olympia. Like many Greek intellectuals of the early nineteenth century, Soutsos expatriated while very young. After studies in Paris and Padua, he moved to Transylvania. When the Greeks won most of southern Greece back from the Ottomans, it become an autonomous nation, after centuries of foreign control. In 1832 the Greeks' allies imposed on them, as their king, a teenage prince from Bavaria. He became Otto I, King of the Hellenes. Soon after Otto arrived at

Nafplio, the first capital of the new nation, the young poet Soutsos moved to Nafplio, too. He soon founded a newspaper there, naming it *The Sun*.

Here he published some poems which he wrote to celebrate the birth of the new Greek nation. The years under Turkish rule had left Greece well behind modern nineteenth-century Europe. Greece had not shared in Western Europe's Renaissance period, nor its Enlightenment. The infrastructure of Greece, its institutions, and its government were in a miserable condition. Like many Greeks after him, Soutsos felt the heavy burden of ancient Greek glory on his new nation. His poetry pointedly asks how modern Greece can gain respect in the modern world, live up to the lofty reputation it had enjoyed in the mind of Western man for centuries.

Some Greeks wanted to emulate successful modern nations such as France, but Soutsos clearly saw that Greece could not suddenly catch up and jump to the top of the new world order. He decided that Greece should seek to restore its *ancient* glory. In Soutsos' 1833 poem "Dialogues of the Dead," the ghost of Plato gazes up from the underworld. He surveys his tattered native land in dismay. He wonders aloud if he is really looking at Greece, and addresses the new nation: "Where are all your great theaters and marble statues?" Plato's ghost asks, "*Where are your Olympic Games?*" (Soutsos 1834: 15; Young 1996: 3). In antiquity the Olympic Games symbolized excellence and prestige, a focal point for all of Greek culture (see chapter 12). Soutsos chose the Olympics here to symbolize all the best features of ancient Greece. That includes the theaters and the art. Soutsos had the broad cultural view of what the games represent.

Soutsos liked ghosts. In his next poem, the ghost of the ancient war hero Leonidas explicitly advises the new Greece to revive its Olympic Games. This idea of restoring antiquity by restoring the Olympics began to take root in Soutsos' very psyche. He took the bold next step: he converted his ghosts' poetic idea into a real-life proposal. In 1835 he sent a long memo to the government, proposing that Greece revive the ancient Olympic Games as an emblem and part of its new independence.

Otto agreed to a great national festival with contests in industry, agriculture, and ancient Greek athletic games. But he did nothing about it. In 1842 Soutsos put his proposal in print and in public, pleading to his king: "Let the ancient Olympic Games be revived in Athens."

I want to emphasize what the young poet's idea really was. It was not just an antiquarian idea, where some modern games would bear the ancient name. Soutsos wanted to revive the games as a step in restoring all of ancient Greece. He wanted to resurrect a dead civilization; he actually sought to revivify time. He kept at it. In 1845 he gave a ringing speech to an Athens crowd of thousands, again urging that the Olympics be revived. But it was a lonely campaign, which he carried on all by himself. Nobody else seemed to care about reviving the Olympics. Even to Greeks of that time, it seemed an odd idea. Yet after twenty years, Soutsos still would not give up; he just kept pushing his revival concept. And finally, in 1856, someone else did care.[1]

Evangelis Zappas was a veteran of the Greek War of Independence. A truly extraordinary, even enigmatic person, he was born to Greek parents in southern Albania. In the 1850s he lived in Romania, where he had become one of the richest men in Eastern Europe, with vast land holdings and many other enterprises. He never set foot in Athens, nor near it. But he learned of Soutsos' Olympic idea and he liked it. He liked it so much that in 1856 he too asked the Greek government to revive the Olympics in Athens. But this time Zappas said that he, Zappas, would pay for it all.

King Otto gave Zappas' Olympic proposal to his foreign minister, Alexandros Rangavis, who thought athletics would be a throwback to primitive bygone times. Athletics, he said, were simply not done in the modern world. In 1856 he was right. Athletics, as we know them, are mainly the invention of the later nineteenth century. When Zappas proposed an Olympic revival in 1856, there were no such athletics anywhere, unless one counts some cricket and rowing contests in England (see chapter 1). So Rangavis suggested to Zappas that agricultural and industrial contests be held instead. The two men reached a compromise, and in 1858 the first modern Olympiad was announced for Athens, 1859. There would be industrial and agricultural Olympics; but Zappas would also have his athletic Olympics, a revival of the games of ancient Greece. On that he insisted. He promised cash prizes for the winners.

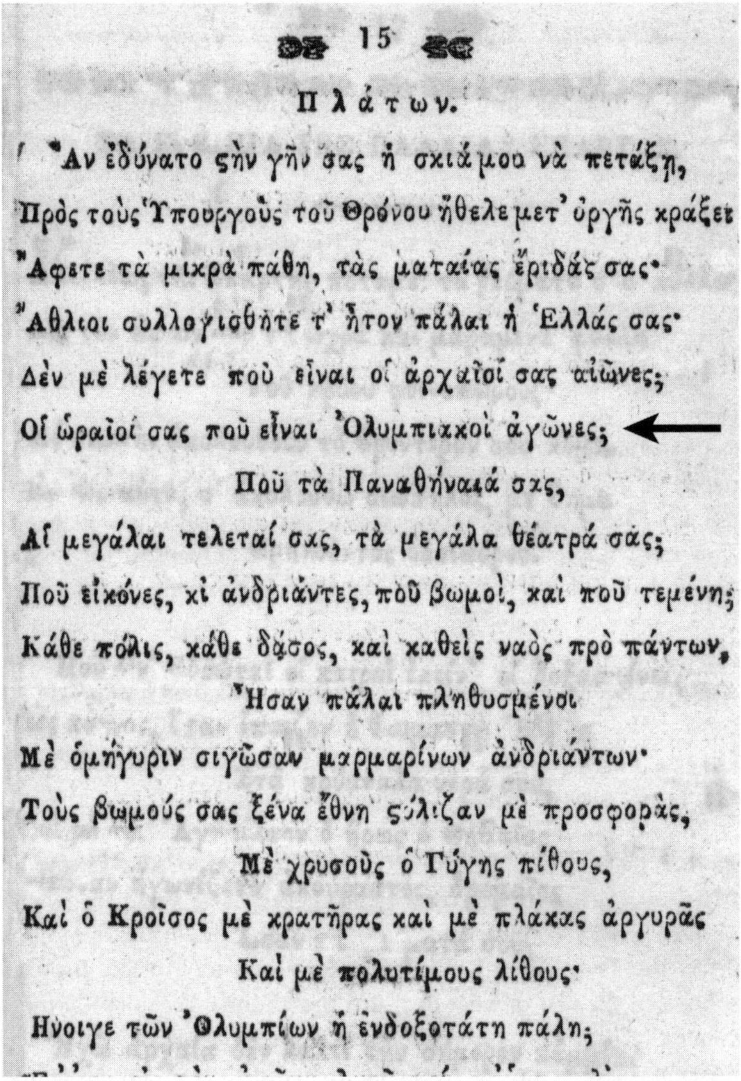

◘§ 15 ◙⊄

Π λ ά τ ων.

΄Αν ἐδύνατο ςὴν γῆϽ σας ἡ σκιά μου νὰ πετάξῃ,
Πρὸς τοὺς Ὑπουργοὺς τοῦ Θρόνου ἤθελε μετ᾿ ὀργῆς κράζει
΄Αφετε τὰ μικρὰ πάθη, τὰς ματαίας ἔριδάς σας·
΄Αθλιοι συλλογισθῆτε τ᾿ ἦτον πάλαι ἡ Ἑλλάς σας·
Δὲν μὲ λέγετε ποὺ εἶναι οἱ ἀρχαῖοί σας αἰῶνες;
Οἱ ὡραῖοί σας ποὺ εἶναι Ὀλυμπιακοὶ ἀγῶνες;   ⟵
              Ποῦ τὰ Παναθήναιά σχς,
Αἱ μεγάλαι τελεταί σχς, τὰ μεγάλα θέατρά σάς;
Ποῦ εἰκόνες, χὶ ἀνδριάντες, ποῦ βωμοὶ, καὶ ποῦ τεμένη;
Κάθε πόλις, κάθε δάσος, καὶ καθεὶς ναὸς πρὸ πάντων,
              ΄Ησαν πάλαι πληθυσμένοι
Μὲ ὁμήγυριν σιγῶσαν μαρμαρίνων ἀνδριάντων·
Τοὺς βωμούς σας ξένα ἔθνη ςὐλιζαν μὲ προσφοράς,
              Μὲ χρυσοὺς ὁ Γύγης πίθους,
Καὶ ὁ Κροῖσος μὲ κρατῆρας καὶ μὲ πλάκας ἀργυρᾶς
              Καὶ μὲ πολυτίμους λίθους·
Ηνοιγε τῶν Ὀλυμπίων ἡ ἐνδοξοτάτη πάλη;

Figure 13.2 Soutsos' 1833 poem, first stage of his revival movement

W. P. Brookes, England, and the First Zappas Olympiad

Suddenly, Olympic history took a wonderful, fateful turn. Without this almost incredible turn of events, I doubt there would be any Olympic Games at all today. It is just a little newspaper clipping – but it is the key, I think, that unlocks the mystery as to how Soutsos' original idea could lead, by direct descent, to Athens 2004. The missing link between Soutsos and Coubertin, between the Zappas Games and Athens 1896, even Athens 2004 and Beijing 2008, is an English doctor named W. P. Brookes. Brookes lived and practiced medicine in a small rural village in Shropshire called Wenlock (figure 13.3).

In the autumn of 1858 Dr. Brookes was reading his local news-paper when a small item caught his eye. This brief article concerned the new Greek Olympics that were to take place at Athens in 1859. This news interested Brookes so much that he clipped the article out and pasted it – just a few inches long – in one of his scrap-books, where it remains for viewing to this day. Brookes kept numer-ous newspaper clippings in his scrapbooks, and all his personal correspondence, even handwritten copies of his own letters sent to others. His meticulous records of all his activities prove that our Olympic movement is a *single, continuous* movement – from Soutsos' first poetic idea to Sydney 2000 and beyond.

Brookes had already started to hold annual village games on a modest scale, which he even called "Meetings of the Olympian Class," because he admired ancient Greece. Now, fired up by the news of Athens' coming games, in July 1859, more than two months *before* the 1859 Athens Olympics themselves took place, Brookes sponsored the first of what he called the "Annual Wenlock Olympic Games." These games were more ambitious, with a much-expanded program, and far greater Hellenic influence than in any "Meeting of the Olympian Class."

Brookes had caught Olympic fever from Soutsos and Zappas. He immediately wrote to the British consul in Athens, wanting to find out more about the coming Athens Olympics. And he sent the Greek organizing committee ten pounds British sterling to be a prize for one of the victors. *Before* the 1859 Olympiad, the Athens

Figure 13.3   W. P. Brookes, the "missing link" between Soutsos and Coubertin

committee announced that, besides the drachma prizes from Zappas, there would be an extra prize from "the Wenlock Olympic Committee of England." Meanwhile, *The Sun* carried article after ecstatic article praising Zappas, the coming Olympics, and what Soutsos rightly and proudly called the fruition of "my poetic idea."

Zappas had given money to excavate the ancient Panathenaic stadium as a site for these games. But the 1859 athletic Olympics took place instead at the flat city square now called Koumoundourou, on Pireus Street, just north of the Kerameikos. It was then just outside the main city. There were no special arrangements for spectators, who could only stand in one large crowd. In 1860 the Olympic committee published a thorough Official Report, much like those now published by the IOC Olympic host cities. The report reproduced many of the pre-games announcements, the actual results, and other relevant documents, including a copy of a ticket to the 1859 Olympics (figure 13.4). Zappas' and Brookes'

Figure 13.4   Ticket to the 1859 (Zappas) Olympics in Athens

cash prizes were indeed awarded. But the games themselves were no great success: the committee had favored the industrial contests over the athletic events.

The program was small, and the athletes had barely trained. Only the front row of the standing spectators could see the events, and those behind them pushed and shoved so that at one point a policeman harshly drove them back. In the featured distance race, the leading runner collapsed and died. Petros Velissariou of Smyrna passed him and won the race – and Brookes' British pounds. Newspaper reporters stressed the flaws of these games, but expressed their hope that the next Olympiad would be better. But the next Olympiad was slow to come.

Otto was driven out of Greece in 1862, replaced by another unemployed royal teenager, a Dane who became George the First. In 1865 Zappas died. He left his fortune to Greece for the Olympics. He also left a rather baffling will. The will stipulated that he was to be buried first at his estate in Romania. After one Olympiad, four years, his body was to be exhumed, and severed at the neck. The main skeleton (the bones below the neck) was to be reburied in his native village in Albania. The head was to be sent to Athens and encased in the new Olympic building there. Zappas gave money for this building, assuming that it would be built within the four-year span. Yet it was not built then, and the entire Soutsos–Zappas Olympic movement in Greece fell into a long hiatus.

Now it was Brookes' turn. In the 1860s Brookes carried on this Olympic movement in *his* country. When he learned the results of the 1859 Athens Olympiad, he had them translated, typeset, and distributed around England. Then he sent a letter to Petros Velissariou, the man who had won the Wenlock prize. It informed Velissariou that he had been elected the "first Honorary Member of the Wenlock Olympic Society." He also sent greetings to N. Theocharis, head of the Greek Olympic Committee. Velissariou's reply graciously thanked Brookes for the honorary membership. Theocharis' letter calls Brookes' Olympic committee and his own in Greece "sister committees united by the same name and a common goal." This exchange of letters proves that there was, back in 1860, a small beginning of an international Olympic movement, even if very brief and embryonic.

This contact with Greece again spurred Brookes on, first to expand his local project to countywide Olympics, and soon to think in even grander terms; namely, National Olympic Games, which would draw athletes and spectators from all of Britain. The First National Olympic Games actually took place in 1866 in London. They were a great success, with many good athletes and 10,000 spectators in London's large indoor arena, the Crystal Palace, the ancestor of all our great covered sporting facilities. But not everyone wished the Olympic movement success.

In class-conscious England, some men of the upper class opposed Brookes' Olympic policy that allowed everyone to compete, even those from the working class. These self-styled aristocrats started a counter-Olympic group called the Amateur Athletic Club, or AAC, and gave the first definition of an amateur athlete: it declared that men who were "mechanics, artisans, or laborers" were *de facto* "professionals," barred from all amateur contests. Amateurism was reserved for "gentlemen," that is, people who did no labor for a living.

Members of this AAC generally boycotted Brookes' Olympics. A few competed in the London 1866 games, and some even won.

But in the 1867 and 1868 editions of the National Olympics, AAC athletes generally abstained. They even published a rule that men who took part in contests with "professionals" could not compete in any contest recognized by the AAC. This rule was directed at the National Olympics and Brookes' policy of accepting working-class entries. Since the members of the AAC also belonged to the power structure in Victorian England, they soon ran the Olympic movement aground. By 1869 Brookes had to give it up, for athletes wanting to compete elsewhere in England could not enter the Olympic Games.

England and Greece, Back and Forth and Back and . . .

Yet then the Olympic ball just bounced back into the Greeks' court. King George announced an end to the long hiatus: a renewed Zappas Olympic series to start in 1870. Now *Greece* preserved the Olympic revival movement. For the 1870 games the committee acquired and excavated the ancient Panathenaic stadium. It could not install the marble seats that Zappas had paid for, but wooden bleachers let about 30,000 satisfied spectators watch a very successful Olympiad. So large a crowd is astonishing for the times. Athletes from all points of the Greek world came to compete, from Crete to Constantinople. If they could not afford the trip, the committee met the cost, letting everyone qualified compete. Several victors were, in fact, from the working class. The wrestling victor was an ordinary manual laborer from Crete. The 200 meter winner was a butcher from Athens.

There were more events and athletes in 1870 than in 1859, and everything was much better organized. All went exceptionally well, and newspaper reports were glowingly favorable. One said the games were "like those of the ancients." Everyone except a few professors at the university judged the games a big success. These professors objected to the working-class victories. Wanting to emulate England's elitist system, they soon gained control of the Olympic Committee. For the next Olympiad, 1875, the new committee simply excluded the working class by declaring everyone ineligible except university students. The 1875 games were far inferior to the 1870 edition in every way. This time the newspapers censured both the committee and the athletes. No more Athens Olympics would even be announced until 1888.

In early 1888 the expensive Olympic Building, now called the Zappeion, was finally completed, and the Olympic Committee announced a special Olympiad for autumn of that year, to celebrate the opening of the new building. Zappas' head was sent down from Romania and encased in the Zappeion. It remains there still today in the central courtyard, behind a plaque which reads, in ancient Greek: "Here lies the head of Evangelis Zappas." It was at this time, it seems, that Zappas' body was divided, like Gaul, into three parts. His flesh indeed stayed in Romania, not far from Bucharest. A long epitaph on his elaborate grave stele reads in part: "Yours, Iphitos, is not the only undying fame. From Zappas, too, Greece has Olympic Games . . . This is the tomb of his flesh." Behind the stele, one can still see the trapdoor through which someone retrieved the skeleton. Except for the head, the rest of his bones were then reburied in southern Albania. In the mountainous, now almost uninhabited and inaccessible village of Labova, there is an aging, but still legible, tombstone which bears the message, in Albanian: "Here lie the bones of the philanthropist Evangelis Zappas."[2]

The Athens Olympic Committee announced that there would be athletic games in the stadium as part of the special 1888 Olympiad, and even listed the exact events to be held. But after this initial announcement, it did absolutely nothing to prepare for or hold the athletic portion of the program. The athletic contests of the 1888 games were tacitly cancelled.[3] It appeared that the Olympic Committee, fully under control of the anti-athletic faction, had killed the real Olympic revival.

Now it was up to Brookes again to keep it alive. The movement just would not die. Several times in the 1870s Brookes had tried again to hold more British National Olympic Games, but apathy and opposition stymied him. He turned to writing articles urging that physical education be taught in the government schools. Yet in the 1880s, as Greece built the Zappeion, Brookes' Olympic dreams returned in changed dress. If he could not gain support in England, perhaps he could get it elsewhere. Whenever blocked, Brookes seems always to have just thought bigger. In 1880 he formally proposed that there be international Olympic Games. And he pointed out the one obvious place for them to be held. He expressed the hope to see the athletes of various nations "contending in a generous rivalry with athletes of other nations in the time-consecrated stadium at Athens" (Young 1996: 60).

This 1880 Athens proposal was the first time that international Olympics had ever been suggested (Coubertin was still a teenage schoolboy). Brookes' own National Olympics allowed, even encouraged, foreign entries; yet they always retained "National" in their name. The Greek series sought from the start to restore to the new Greece what were its national games in antiquity. Brookes' international Olympic revival idea was soon published in both Greek and English newspapers. He asked the Greek ambassador in London, John Gennadius, to help rally the Greek government behind his Athens plan. Over the next decade, Brookes wrote a dozen letters to Gennadius, but with no result. Perhaps the anti-athletic Greek Olympic Committee advised Gennadius to quash the Englishman's zeal. With no support from English athletic clubs, his best shot, his international proposal, went nowhere.

The French Connection

Toward the end of the 1880s Brookes resumed his other obsession, to establish physical education in his country's schools. At the same time, a young French nobleman and Anglophile, Baron Pierre de Coubertin, became similarly obsessed with such a project in France. In his own speeches, he began to quote Brookes' writings on the subject. Then he wrote to Brookes asking if he could visit him to discuss their common interest.

Coubertin arrived in Wenlock in October 1890. Brookes held a special edition of his Wenlock Olympic Games in his honor. He also asked the baron to plant a tree there. Brookes loved trees. Trees appear throughout his writings, and trees still ring the field where he held his Wenlock Olympic Games. He hoped his Olympic idea might grow and expand in the same way as his trees, which he always saw as symbols of ever increasing and lasting progress.

Then Brookes took Coubertin into his trophy room. There, in the trophy room, Coubertin himself wrote, Brookes showed him the victors' list from the 1859 Zappas Olympics; and accounts of the 1866 London Olympics. He showed him 1881 newspapers reporting his own proposals for starting international Olympic Games in Athens. Yet years later Coubertin actually stated in print that there had never been any Zappas Olympics at all, and pretended that he knew nothing of Brookes' own Olympic endeavors (Coubertin 1908: 108, 53; 1932 [Brookes' name omitted]; Young 1996: 235, n. 16).

In 1888 Coubertin had ridiculed the idea of modern Olympic Games when it was proposed by another Frenchman. So also, when he returned to Paris from Wenlock in 1890, he belittled Brookes' idea of reviving the Olympic Games, writing "there was no need to invoke memories of Greece" (1986: 1.111 [1888] France; 1890: 712 Brookes; Young 1996: 74, 82). Yet by 1892 he had somehow wholly changed his mind. He himself suddenly made a public proposal for an Olympic revival, maintaining that it was a novel idea, and all his own.

There was action in Greece, too. The Crown Prince Constantine had announced the government would sponsor a revival of the Zappas series for that same year, 1892. But financial and political problems prevented it. Brookes kept writing in vain to Gennadius, because Coubertin had not told him of his own revival proposal. In fact the baron did not even answer Brookes' letters any more.

What Coubertin *did* do was plan for an International Athletic Congress in Paris in June 1894. He was slow in sending out invitations, so that Europeans received no invitation until the month before the Congress. Brookes received one – a mere form letter – and wrote to Coubertin wishing him success in his Olympic enterprise. He also sent a letter to the prime minister of Greece, Charilaos Trikoupis. The letter reminded Trikoupis of Brookes' own earlier connections with the Zappas Games, and ended this way: "My friend Pierre de Coubertin, myself, and others are endeavoring to promote international Olympic festivals. I hope your King will patronize such Games." Thus Brookes saw Coubertin and himself linked together as Olympic advocates.

When the delegates arrived at the Sorbonne to attend Coubertin's conference, which was originally named a "Congress of Amateurs," the baron had renamed it "Congress for the Revival of the Olympic Games." This 1894 Paris congress lasted several days. The delegates were wined, dined and entertained in grand style. Coubertin soon held the delegates in his hands. No one opposed his moves to form an international Olympic committee to revive the ancient games. He planned to have the first games in Paris, 1900. Somehow the date got accelerated by four years, to 1896. But the delegates did not at first vote for Athens as the 1896 site. They chose London. Strangely, the Anglophile Coubertin refused to support London. He nominated Athens instead, and insisted on it. When it was clear the London motion would pass anyway, Coubertin had the whole question postponed, "tabled" (Coubertin 1894: minutes for June 19).

The choice of Athens for 1896 remains mostly a mystery. Coubertin was unquestionably the first to nominate Athens. At that same June 19 meeting, Demetrios Vikelas was elected president of that sub-committee, to his great surprise. Vikelas was a Greek intellectual who lived in Paris. He was a fascinating man of diverse talents: a novelist, a historian – he even translated Shakespeare into Greek. But he had never before had a thing to do with athletics. At first Vikelas did not himself support the baron's nomination of Greece, but that evening he changed his mind. Four days later, at a plenary meeting on the last day of the Congress, Vikelas himself made a second, more formal and far more successful proposal for Athens' candidacy. In the meantime, he had communicated with people in Athens. Vikelas' Athens proposal was approved by acclamation. Vikelas was chosen the first president of the IOC, preceding Coubertin and all the rest, such as Brundage, Samaranch, and now Rogge.

Although he had never had a thing to do with any athletic organization, Vikelas was the right man for the job. In the autumn of 1894 Coubertin and Vikelas visited Athens briefly and separately. It was Coubertin's first visit to Greece.[4] Both men met opposition from the Greek government and from the members of the Zappas Olympic Committee, each group claiming that they could not help and that Olympic Games were impossible. There was no money, they said, "No way." Vikelas returned to Athens in December. Coubertin suddenly got engaged to be married and started to write a history book. He lost much of his interest in the 1896 games.

When Stephanos Dragoumis, president of the Zappas Olympic Committee, again emphatically told Vikelas "No," Prince Constantine offered to chair the organizing committee. In early 1895 Vikelas and Constantine rallied other Greeks behind their efforts. Vikelas gave speeches to labor union assemblies, and Constantine formed special committees for each sport. In parliament pro-Olympic Greeks invoked the tradition of the Zappas Games, and said that these international Olympics would fulfill Zappas' dream. That argument won, the government changed, the Zappas committee stepped aside, and Athens began preparing feverishly for 1896. Vikelas and the other Greeks did almost all of the work. Coubertin did very little.

The Athens organizing committee somehow achieved amazing success. There were no previous international Olympiads to serve as models. Very few foreign teams or athletes committed to – or even heard about – the new Olympics. There was, however, a great in-flux of good will and donations for the cause from Greeks both in Greece and abroad. Even peasants in the villages sent a few drachmas to Athens. Giorgos Averoff, an Egyptian Greek, paid to restore the ancient Panathenaic stadium, with magnificent marble seats.

Unfortunately, Brookes did not live to see his own Olympic dream fulfilled. He died just three months before those 1896 games took place, joining Soutsos and Zappas in Olympic oblivion – as Coubertin and history forgot all about them. Even Gennadius had amnesia. Just before the games, he published an article praising Coubertin for his brilliant and original idea of an Olympic revival. The article makes no mention at all of W. P. Brookes, whom Gennadius had rebuffed repeatedly when Brookes had advocated the same plan.

The 1896 games themselves, against all odds, despite truly miserable weather, were an astonishing success. The big stadium, the first in the modern world, overflowed with the largest crowd ever to witness a sporting event. *Everyone* observed virtually perfect decorum. Americans won most events in the stadium, and the Greeks applauded strongly, as they did for every winning athlete. Yet they were burning to win an event themselves in the stadium, in front of the crowd. Greece was favored to win the discus and the shot put. In both events, however, the best Greek athletes finished a tiny fraction of an inch behind the American, Garrett.

Greatly disappointed, the Greeks still applauded him. But it seemed almost as if the Olympian gods had abandoned them.

All thoughts, all Greek hopes now rested with the marathon, a wholly new event to be held for the first time (see appendix C). The hype the day before the race was immense. Businessmen promised great rewards to the winner – if he was Greek. Even unbelievers prayed that the marathon victory go to Greece. As the afternoon of marathon day wore on, all other events were finished except the pole vault, which was suddenly interrupted. It seemed the stadium had gone mad.

"It's a Greek, it's a Greek," the crowd shouted in one voice. It was indeed a Greek, Spyros Loúis, who entered the stadium first. The joy that filled the air, reports say, was indescribable. Almost all eyewitnesses, including Coubertin, even many years later, state that it was one of the most memorable sights of their entire lives, truly unforgettable (Young and Bijkerk: 1999). In short, it seems as if Greece had been born again through the victory of this one young man.

These 1896 Olympic Games were so successful that almost everyone except Coubertin wanted Greece to be the permanent seat of all future Olympiads. But Greece itself fell into very hard times – the euphoria of the games was punctured by financial losses and military disasters. The Greeks could not oppose Coubertin's plans for 1900 in Paris. But the Paris 1900 Olympiad was a big flop. The French government would not cooperate, nor let the games be called Olympics. Athletes from around the world did compete sporadically on the outskirts of Paris. There were no crowds of spectators, and apparently most athletes did not even know they were in Olympics. It was a total failure. The next Olympiad was given to America, and ended up as an appendage to the 1904 St. Louis World's Fair. The games were not truly international; almost all the athletes were North American. Attendance was poor, organization abysmal, and sometimes even perverse.

Greece and Sweden Save the Day

After two such fiascoes the Olympics might well have died in the cradle, if Greece had not come to the aid of the faltering institution. There had been an agreement, against Coubertin's wishes, that Athens would hold international Olympics in between the games that moved around the world. Greece was in no position to plan to hold these in-between games for their first scheduled date, 1902. But in 1901 the rest of the IOC members voted, against Coubertin's strong objections, to sanction IOC games at Athens in 1906. Before these games Coubertin was compelled to recognize them in his Olympic journal, but he did not attend. Others of the IOC, who had supported the project all along, had a business meeting there anyway.

In 1906 Athens indeed hosted its second official IOC Olympiad. Like the first, it was a total success, but a lot bigger, with large numbers of spectators and athletes from many more nations. There was good will and satisfaction among all.

Several important features of our Olympics today were inaugurated at the 1906 Olympiad. It was the first time the athletes paraded around the stadium grouped by nation in an opening ceremony; the first time that all athletes were sent by a national Olympic committee and officially represented their countries. These and other innovations of 1906 were repeated at subsequent Olympiads, and are now among our most characteristic and venerable Olympic traditions (Lennartz 2001: 20–7).

Most Olympic historians agree that in 1906 Greece probably saved Coubertin's revival movement from early extinction. But Coubertin, always loath to give Greece any credit for the success of the revival movement, declared that the 1906 games were not sanctioned by the IOC and were "unofficial." This designation has remained with the second Athens Olympiad because for many years Coubertin *was* the IOC and the only other president before World War II was an old crony of his. After the war there was an organized attempt to restore their IOC recognition to the 1906 games, but IOC president Avery Brundage nearly worshipped Coubertin and would have none of it. Early in 2003 the International Society of Olympic Historians submitted to IOC president Rogge a well documented petition asking that the 1906 games be redesignated "Official" IOC games. It was signed by many of the world's most distinguished Olympic scholars. But for over half a century one of the major functions of the IOC has been to enhance and preserve Coubertin's image in history. Apparently intimidated either by IOC tradition or by the ghost of Coubertin, Rogge denied the scholars' petition, and history along with it. Thus, in 2003, the IOC continued to deny its own decision of 1901, and the official 1906 Athens Olympiad remains officially unofficial.

The 1908 Olympics had already been scheduled for Rome. But in 1906, for several reasons, the Italians backed out of their commitment. Perhaps it all might have ended there. But emboldened by Athens' recent success, London, once the bastion of Olympic opposition, offered to replace Rome even at such short notice. The 1908 London Games were good in some ways, bad in others. But they were much better than the 1900 and 1904 fiascoes. And coupled with the excellent games of 1906, the London Olympiad seemed to stabilize the institution well enough that it was no longer moribund.

The Stockholm games of 1912 were then and are still known as the "Jim Thorpe Olympics." This highly talented and unassuming Native American performed such amazing feats of excellence that newspapers spread his name and achievements all around the world. The Thorpe story made fascinating reading, and it was the first time that an Olympiad had received so much favorable publicity. Some think that Jim Thorpe saved the struggling Olympic movement almost as much as Athens 1906.

Epilogue and Encore

When the highly successful Stockholm games in 1912 seemed to assure a future for the movement, Greece was already planning for its in-between Olympics of 1914. And several countries, including the USA, announced that they would again send teams to Athens. But by 1914 the game had changed – changed from sport to the horrors of World War I. To his great credit, Coubertin somehow kept the IOC and the Olympic movement alive throughout the war, so that the games could resume relatively intact in Antwerp in 1920. Except for another war casualty in 1940 and 1944 they have continued every four years since then, becoming bigger and better virtually every time.

As the games are international, so was their creation. The modern games have not just one founder; at least five men were indispensable: a Frenchman, an Englishman, and three Greeks. They are, namely, Soutsos, Zappas, Brookes, Coubertin, and Vikelas. When we fully understand the motive behind Soutsos' original proposal and the chain of events it set in motion, it is clear that our modern Olympics are an authentic continuation of their ancient namesake.

The games have undergone astounding changes since they left Greece in 1906. The changes are not so much changes in essence, but changes in size and scope. The modern Olympic Games have survived, despite amateurism, world wars, cold war, political meddling, and boycotts. And they continue to grow. The ancient Olympics endured more than a millennium of comparable hardships, slowly expanding in their events, competitors, and importance as their world slowly expanded. They were intended for all people, not just the elite. Even if seldom realized, their goal was to bring together in peace the world's best athletes in friendly competition in the pursuit of human excellence. With each of our modern Olympiads, the best athletes from all over our world gather to recreate that original Olympic goal. And the games get rapidly bigger and bigger, as our own world expands more and more rapidly. Brookes' tree image looks all the more apt.

In 1890 the oak which Brookes and Coubertin planted together in Wenlock Field was just a sapling, still small and thin. Inevitably, at first its growth was slow. Each year it has grown, always spreading out more, almost exponentially, with more and more branches, a thicker trunk, and ever more sturdy limbs. It just keeps on growing and growing, as do the Olympics. It now towers high above the visitor, and today its wide branches make a kind of huge umbrella.

On one occasion, Brookes abandoned the tree as a symbol for what he hoped the Olympic movement would become (Young 1996: 39). But he still focused on natural growth:

> Sow a single seed of a rare plant in the most secluded spot and if the soil and other conditions are favourable . . . it will grow up and bear another seed, and in time, produce plants sufficient to cover the length and breadth of the land.

As we watch the games in Beijing in 2008, we can be assured that the "breadth of the land" in these prophetic words is a metaphor for this whole wide world.

APPENDIX A

Chronology and Schedule of the Athletic Circuit

Chronology

The Ancient World is an inclusive term, encompassing many centuries of civilization, and several distinct places and cultures. This study is restricted to the Greco-Roman world, which is ordinarily divided into distinct periods of time. In general, these distinctions are based on changes determined more by archaeology and art than by literary or cultural trends, but even those distinctions are rather arbitrary. Nevertheless, because changes took place over so vast a time, a chronological breakdown is unquestionably useful. That given below is probably more arbitrary and approximate than most, because a more detailed version is not needed for the purposes of this book, and might even confuse. I have added a few remarks in parentheses. All times before the Archaic period are considered "prehistorical," in that they precede any evidence for writing in the Greek alphabet. Unless specified AD, all dates below are BC.

Bronze Age	2,500–1,100 BC
Mycenaean Age	1600–1100
Greek Dark Ages	1100–776 (776: founding of Olympic Games)
Archaic period	776 (Homer sometime between 760 and 700)
Early	776–650 (from 750 approximately)
Middle	650–550

Late	550–480 or 500 (about 550–450: golden century of Greek athletics)

Classical period	480–323
Early	480–440 (480–479: Persian Wars end)
Middle	440–380
Late	380–323 (323: death of Alexander the Great)

Post-Classical ("Rather Late")

Hellenistic	323–146 (146: Roman army destroys Corinth, Greece)
Roman Republic	146–1 BC/1 AD (division at 1 is for convenience only; Augustus – first emperor – sole ruler, 30 BC–14 AD)
Roman Empire	1 AD–500/600 AD
	Early 1–100 AD
	Middle 100–200 AD
	Late 200–400 AD (Christian emperor outlaws pagan festivals shortly before and/ or after 400 AD)
	End of antiquity: 500 AD (Western Roman Empire, 600: Eastern Empire becomes Byzantine Empire)

Mediaeval	500–1400 AD (all dates here very approximate)
Dark Ages	500–1000 AD
Late Mediaeval	1000–1400 AD

The Renaissance period follows the Mediaeval period (except in Greece, under Ottoman rule); then comes the Modern period in general.

Schedule of the Circuit: The Four Major Athletic Festivals

Festival	Place	Founded	God honored	Frequency
Olympics	Olympia	776 BC	Zeus	Every four years
Pythians	Delphi	582 BC	Apollo	Every four years

| Isthmians | Isthmia | 582 BC | Poseidon | Every two years |
| Nemeans | Nemea | 573 BC | Zeus | Every two years |

Five year example:

476 Olympics
475 Nemeans and Isthmians
474 Pythians
473 Nemeans and Isthmians
472 Olympics

Technical Note on Discus and Long Jump

Since I have taken a position here contrary to prevailing opinion on how these two events were executed, some readers may want to know why I diverge from what they may read elsewhere.

Discus

Gardiner (1930: 157–8) and Swaddling (1980: 51), among others, maintain that the throw was made mainly with arm strength, without the full rotation of the body which modern discus throwers use to create centrifugal force. And in the most recent scholarly study, Langdon also has vigorously argued that no spin of the body took place (Langdon 1990: 177–80). In the end, however, I think Langdon's argument and all the evidence which he cites are far from conclusive. Perhaps some ancient artists occasionally sacrifice exact reality to artistic gain, but they are not so incompetent that we may ignore several artistic witnesses on little grounds other than their failure to fit well with a particular thesis.

Even if Philostratus' detailed description of a discus thrower (*Imagines* 1.24) should prove to be an analysis of Myron's diskobolos statue, like so much of the *Gymnastica*, it is worth almost nothing.[1] He seems never to have seen an actual discus throw, for he even mistakes a statue base for a platform which living athletes must stand on when they throw. And the biomechanical study which

Langdon cites rashly assumes that Myron's statue represents the athlete in the very midst of the throwing movement, although it might well portray a more preliminary move.

Langdon cites three literary passages which mention an athlete's discus throw, and argues that the verb meaning "spin" in each case denotes the spin of the discus, not that of the athlete's body. Yet of these three, *Olympian* 10.72–3 is not really a parallel, because here the object of the participle is the thrower's hand, not the article thrown, a stone (discus – which is here in the *dative* case). The verb (*kyklyo*) may well mean "encircle" as much as "spin."

In Homer's *Odyssey* 8.189–90 and *Iliad* 23.839–40 the thrown article could be the object of the verb "threw" just as easily as the object of the participle meaning "spinning." And in the latter, that article is not a discus, anyway, but the much heavier and probably far from flat *solos*. Langdon himself notes that the verbs in question (*dineo* and [*peri*]*strepho*), even in the active and uncompounded forms, are used intransitively as well as transitively, that is, "spin/whirl" oneself "around" as well as to "spin" something else "around." Therefore I think that the literary evidence may be somewhat ambiguous, but the not nearly so ambiguous artistic evidence decides the case in favor of a body spin.

Long Jump

Sources for the two jumps exceeding 50 feet are as follows:

1 Zenobius (second century AD) quotes a light-hearted epigram (6.23) about how Phayllos (early fifth century BC) jumped 55 feet (so far "that he broke his leg").
2 Africanus' list (third century AD) says that Chionis (sixth century BC) jumped 52 feet. There is no evidence that Chionis ever competed in the pentathlon, and the Armenian translation of the same text reads 22 feet.

Both sources have even further drawbacks too complex to explain here.

Ebert's theory of five sequential standing jumps (1963: 2–34) is followed, for example, by Sinn (2000: 40–1), Drees (1968: 74–5),

Figure B1 Long jumper in midst of his jump; Boston Museum of Fine Arts, 01.8020, r-f kylix, painted by Onesimos

Swaddling (1980: 55–6), and even the tour guides at Olympia. Yet all ancient depictions show the jumpers taking off with one foot, as in our running jump. *Any* standing jumper *must* take off with both feet parallel and closely together, as a simple try or Ebert's own photos of his experiments with a standing jumper confirm far beyond doubt.[2] Yet Ebert simply argues that all the ancient artists drew the pictures wrong. Thus, just as Langdon dismisses art concerning the discus (above), so Ebert rejects the artistic evidence, but even more casually.

Ebert's argument also rests on a claim that no example in Greek art clearly shows a long jumper taking a run. Apart from the lost vase from Apulia (Ebert 1963), and that in Gardiner (1930: figure 101) (both mere line drawings), a vase in Frankfurt, so far ignored here, certainly represents a jumper running with the weights. The standard catalog of vases shows a photograph of it (*CVA* Germany 30, plate 68: r-f bowl, last half of fifth century).

Several ancient paintings capture a jumper in precisely the same high mid-air position as our own running jumpers have at the apex of their jump: legs forward, almost parallel to the ground. As Ebert's own photos indisputably indicate, a standing jumper never achieves the height or leg extension shown on these ancient paintings. Therefore if we *reject* the two very late, clearly erroneous reports of jumps beyond 50 feet, *all* ancient art and even the rest of the literary evidence clearly suggest a single, running jump, much the same as ours. Gardiner (1904) long ago gave excellent and cogent reasons to reject them (cf. Gardiner 1910: 309–10; 1930: 153).

APPENDIX C

Modern Issues: The Marathon and Torch Relay

The Marathon Race

The famous battle of Marathon took place in 490 BC, during the first of two Persian invasions of Greece. A mainly Athenian Greek force of 10,000 troops defeated a much larger invading Persian army, and drove the Persians from Greek soil. Just a few decades later the historian Herodotus, by far the most reliable source, recounts Athens' attempt to enlist Sparta's aid against these barbarians (6.105). The Athenians sent a runner named Philippides to Sparta, asking for its assistance. (It is important to note here that some manuscripts give the runner's name as Pheidippides, instead.) The Spartans agreed, but delayed their departure several days in order to complete a religious festival. They arrived at Marathon the day after the battle. There is no mention here of *any* runner being sent to Athens to announce the great victory at Marathon. Philippides' run to Sparta, however, was much longer than any route from Marathon to Athens (perhaps up to 150 miles compared with scarcely more than 25 miles).

Several athletes, too, according to ancient sources, ran non-stop farther than the Marathon–Athens distance. After he won the distance race at Olympia in 328 BC, Ageus of Argos, Africanus reports, ran straight to his homeland to announce his success, and he arrived on the same day. So also a fourth century inscription claims that an Argive runner named Drymos ran all the way from Olympia to Epidaurus in a single day, and announced his Olympic victory there (*IG* iv.1349).

Pausanias saw the tomb of the distance runner Ladas near Sparta (3.21). He says that Ladas "apparently" died after running all the way from Olympia right after his victory (about 460 BC). Each of these three athletes would have covered about 100 miles or more in a single day, a distance which seems unlikely. Whatever the validity of these reports, they nevertheless attest to a genre of tale in which an athlete completes a long run to announce his victory. And the story of Ladas who died after a long run may have inspired later reports of military couriers' similar fatal efforts.

Plutarch, in the late first century AD, claims that after the battle of Plataea (480 BC), a man named Euchidas ran from Plataea to Delphi to fetch some of its holy fire. He returned to Plataea the same day, but dropped dead on his arrival, just as he handed the fire over to the Plataean citizens (*Aristides* 20.5). Elsewhere, Plutarch tells a somewhat similar tale connected to the battle of Marathon, which may well be a spin-off of the same story. He states that a man named Eukles – "or some say Thersippos" – an Athenian participant in the battle at Marathon in 490 BC, "still in his armor," ran to Athens and forthwith died just as he announced news of the victory to the Athenian leaders (*Moralia* 347C).

A century after Plutarch, the satirist and essayist Lucian conflated virtually the same story with Herodotus' original account of Philippides' run to Sparta, but he uses the alternate name. "Pheidippides," Lucian declares, ran from Marathon to Athens and just as he uttered the words, "Rejoice, we won," he dropped dead. Thus the first version of the Marathon story as we know it dates from the late second century AD, more than seven centuries after the battle itself.

Robert Browning's 1878 poem "Pheidippides" made the story of the purported run from Athens to Marathon famous. His Pheidippides breaks in on the group of leaders at Athens and shouts: "'Rejoice, we conquer!' Like wine through clay, / Joy in his blood bursting his heart, he died – the bliss!"

Browning's poem immediately became popular, not only in England but also on the Continent. Obviously inspired by the dramatic story of Pheidippides, the Frenchman Michel Bréal convinced Coubertin to incorporate into the 1896 Athens program an actual race that would mirror Pheidippides' feat. That first marathon race, won by Spyros Louis of Greece, was one of the most memorable events in the history of sport (see chapter 13). Each of the next three marathons was unusual, as well, even for so unusual an event. The 1900 marathon took place through the streets of Paris, and foreign athletes complained that only the French runners knew the course – and they took shortcuts. In 1904 the runner who entered the stadium first was soon disqualified for having hitched a ride on a truck along the way. And the 1908 marathon was the most controversial of all. The leading runner, Dorando Pietri of Italy, collapsed just a few yards from the finish line. The British officials lifted him up, dragged him across the line, and declared him the winner. But the protest of the American John Hayes, who finished behind him, succeeded. The Queen of England gave Pietri a duplicate prize, anyway. The race had started at Windsor Castle and finished directly in front of the royal box at the stadium. That exact distance established the official length of all our marathon races today: 26 miles, 385 yards (42.263 kilometers).

The Olympic Torch Relay

The torch relay has become a major feature of the modern Olympics, and is now one of its biggest, most attractive traditions. Now millions of onlookers watch thousands of torchbearers. Yet the route from Olympia to Athens 2004 is the only Olympic torch relay to pass the torch through every continent in the world. Although many people assume that the torch relay somehow derives from a ceremony of the ancient Olympics, there was nothing comparable in antiquity. The modern torch is lit at the ancient temple of Hera, and then relayed to the site of the games. Since the distance from the temple to the stadium was never more than 200 meters, and even shorter in the Archaic and Classical periods, there was no need for – no thought of – a relay in antiquity.[1] The flame at Hera's temple was kept perpetually lit (see chapter 5), but it played no role in the ancient Olympic Games themselves.

The torch relay was the brilliant innovation of Carl Diem, the principal organizer of the 1936 Berlin Olympics. Diem held his

Figure C1 Lighting of torch for relay to Seoul Olympics, 1988; photo by author

Olympic position in Germany long before Hitler and the Nazis came to power. He had earlier been in charge of organizing the 1916 Berlin Olympics, which were cancelled because of World War I. Although the idea of an Olympic torch relay was original with Diem, a few elements in the background made it especially suitable to its purpose.

The humanists of the latter nineteenth and earlier twentieth centuries were fond of representing the transfer of traditions from one generation to the next by the metaphor of "passing the torch." The organizers of the Amsterdam Olympiad in 1928 had hit upon the idea of an Olympic Flame, and the flame burned throughout those games from high up on a special tower on the edge of the stadium. Diem combined the notions of a relay and of a fire, and then added his own inspiration; namely, that the Olympic fire be lit in ancient Olympia (Borgers 1996: 9–28). This link to the past seemed to legitimize the modern Olympics in general; but it also, of course, attracted worldwide attention to the coming 1936 games, which the Nazi regime saw as a great opportunity for disseminating favorable propaganda.

After World War II, when the games resumed at London, the organizers decided to include the torch relay from ancient Olympia. The event took twelve days, and the torch crossed the Adriatic by boat from Corfu to Bari, and the Channel from Calais to Dover. Ever since then, the torch relay has generally become bigger and better, so that now it is one of the most important and revered of all Olympic institutions. Almost all those who have carried the torch claim that the experience left them with an emotional feeling that was immense and unforgettable. Furthermore, the way the torch now readily traverses continents and national boundaries highlights the international character of the Olympics and their power to promote international peace. Diem had a good idea.

Notes

Chapter 1: Introduction

1 Actually only 192.27 meters at Olympia. For this and other technical terms, see the glossary at the back of the book.

2 The first entry for the basic word, *ludus*, in the standard *Latin Dictionary* (Lewis and Short 1958) reads, "In general, a *play, game, diversion, pastime.*" The original (now obsolete) meaning of English "ludicrous" was "playful."

3 If the Pythian Games had just been founded, such elaborate facilities are unlikely for the first Pythiad. Archaeologists have found no trace of the first stadium at Delphi or of any hippodrome. In the early years both were down in the valley, far from the sanctuary of Apollo itself.

Chapter 3: Athletic Events

1 Since the positions which I take here concerning the method of the discus throw and long jump do not conform with the scholarly views which tend now to prevail, appendix B contains a technical assessment of the scholarship and the evidence on which I base my judgment.

Chapter 4: Combat and Equestrian Events

1 The mention of wrestling on the ground, "in the mud" or "in the dirt" at Lucian *Anacharsis* 8, may mislead. Lucian uses the word "wrestling"

here as a generic term that includes the *pancration* (see below), to which this passage certainly refers.

2 Because this result (only one of forty chariots finishing the race) seems unlikely, J. Ebert has vigorously challenged the accuracy of the text in the Pindar manuscripts (Ebert 1989: 98–9). I strongly sympathize with his uneasiness with respect to the text, but do not find his proposed reading (which replaces the number 40 with the number 4) convincing.

3 The Olympic record for most victories in any one event was set by Herodoros of Megara, who won the trumpet in ten successive Olympiads, 328–284 BC.

Chapter 5: Zeus Country

1 Some of the money to finance the building may have had a source other than the Panhellenic donations. Pausanias (5.10.2) says that the Eleans financed the temple with the spoils of yet another war against Pisa. Gardiner (1910: 119) and many others follow this explanation, but it does not rest on solid ground. For example, it creates an insurmountable chronological difficulty within the text of Pausanias itself. As Drees (1968: 114) says, "There is some confusion concerning the events leading up to the erection of the temple." As Levi remarks, "The destruction of Pisa by Elis and the looting of the Pisatan temple are highly problematic events" (1971, II: 23). I think it is far from certain that there were any spoils from Pisa at this time. (The date of this Elis–Pisa war expressed in Herodotus 4.148, "in my time," is too vague to be relevant.)

2 Dio Chrysostom, *Orat.* 12.25; Lucian, *Imag.* 24; Quintilian 12.10.9; *Greek Anthology* 16.81 (Philip of Thessalonike); Arrian, *Diss. Epict.*1.6.

Chapter 6: Pindar and Immortality

1 Recently a few tiny papyrus scraps have come to light which suggest that the somewhat earlier poet Ibycus *may* have written a few *epinician*s before Simonides. There are later victory odes by only two other poets, and they are anomalies in their time, both clearly seeking to recall the tenor of those earlier days of glory (Euripides 755 PMG; Callimachus. frag. T384, 389).

2 In 1979 the Pittsburgh Pirates, led and inspired by Willy Stargell, won Baseball's World Series. After the final game, a television reporter

interviewed him. "How much money did you win, Willy? What's the share each player gets from the winner's purse?" Stargell eyed him as if he were an alien, and replied, softly at first, but in a crescendo. "I don't know how much money I made. Look, man, I play all year to make a living. But this was the World Series. All I wanted to do was do my best against the best. Look, man, I would have played *this one for free!*"

3 Centuries after their death, a few early athletes were classed as "heroes," and even had shrines in their hometowns. But a hero is not the same thing as a god (see chapter 9).

Chapter 8: Questions of Profit and Social Class

1 Full details and copious documentation for all the statements and sources mentioned in this chapter appear in Young (1984); I therefore often forgo documentation that might seem in order here, referring readers to my 1984 book.

2 Kyle (1987: 111–14); Poliakoff (1987: 129–32); Sinn (2000: 30); cf. Golden (1998: 142–4).

3 For the method of calculating a comparable dollar amount in dollars, see Young (1984: 116–26, 128–30). I have doubled those 1980 figures so as to update them to 2001 dollars; a 100 percent increase of the earlier figures accords almost exactly with the US government's figures for inflation between those two years, both in wages and in the cost of living.

Chapter 9: The Athletes

1 For the text of the similar inscription honoring Kleitomachos (who broke Theogenes' Isthmian record), see chapter 4.

Chapter 10: Women and Greek Athletics

1 To render the Greek word *parthenos* into ordinary contemporary English is virtually impossible. The word most apt, "maiden," is obsolescent in contemporary American English. Many translate it as "virgins" (Miller 1991: 101–2), others as "girls" (Drees 1968: 28). The former overemphasizes the sexual status/activity of these young women, but

the latter might suggest too young an age, perhaps even implying that some children could be among the group. "Unmarried girls" and "young women" are slight improvements, but too vague, I think, at least as they might apply in modern contexts. Greek females tended to marry at a much younger age than most Americans and others in Western culture. The *parthenoi* here would have all been teenagers, many in their early to mid teens. Anyone 20 years old would have been an unmarried woman, not an unmarried girl, and probably not viewed as a young woman. I think that "teenage girls," while far from perfect, is the most accurate when clarity could be lost. I also use "girls" and "young women" when the context allows.

Chapter 12: The Later Centuries of Olympia

1   Moses himself is problematic, hardly a reliable source for the ancient Olympics. Today, Armenian historians are not even sure whether he lived in the fifth century AD – or the seventh, or the ninth.

Chapter 13: The Origin and Authenticity of the Modern Olympic Games

1   Young (1996: 4–7). My 1996 book contains all the information given here, and more. Copiously documented, it gives a precise source for every quotation or attributed idea. I therefore forego giving all but the most essential citations here, and refer readers to the documentation in that book.

2   I thank Mihaela Lipetz-Penes, of the Romanian Olympic Committee (gold medalist, javelin, 1964 Olympics), for taking me to Zappas' Romanian tomb; and Paul Zappas of Los Angeles for his photos of the Albanian tomb.

3   The following year, in lieu of the missing 1888 games, a private individual sponsored and financed some games he called "Olympics." They were held inside his tiny gym, with almost no spectators. The few athletes, elite university students, misbehaved so badly that the program was halted in midstream.

4   Coubertin went to Greece only two other times in his life; in 1896 to view the first IOC Olympiad, and in 1927 to receive an award which the Greeks bestowed upon him.

Appendix B: Technical Note on Discus and Long Jump

1   Most think that the Philostratus who wrote this book of *Imagines* is the author of the *Gymnastica*, as well. Yet some believe that the works are by two different men of the same name. (Yet another man of the same name – probably the first man's grandson – wrote yet another work with the same title, *Imagines*; he is called Philostratus *minor*, that is, "Philostratus the younger.")

   Langdon and others (e.g., Gardiner 1930: 155) assume that Philostratus is here analyzing the diskobolos statue sculpted by Myron. They fail to mention that Philostratus, however, explicitly states that he is describing a "painting" (*graphe*), a term hard to reconcile with any assumption that his subject is Myron's statue (and offering poor support for Langdon's preference of Philostratus' wordy second-hand description of a two-dimensional item over the extant and visible "two dimensional" vase paintings, which Langdon rejects as irrelevant).

2   Therefore Gardiner mistook runners in the post-480 starting position (see chapter 3) for jumpers and called them "standing jumpers without weights" (1910: 308; 1930: 144, 151). There were no standing jumpers, either in reality or in the pictures on the vases.

Appendix C: Modern Issues: The Marathon and Torch Relay

1   Before the stadium was moved farther east at the end of the Classical period, the starting line was even closer to the temples. At Athens, a torch race (unrelated to the Olympics) took place as part of a festival in honor of Prometheus, the hero of fire.

Glossary

Altis	The sanctuary portion of the Olympic site, devoted to religious purposes.
Amentum (Latin)	A thong wrapped around a javelin and attached to the fingers. It unravels and imparts a spin to the javelin as it comes off the athlete's hand.
Ankyle (Greek)	Same as *amentum*.
Big Four	The Olympic, Pythian, Isthmian, and Nemean festivals, as a group recognized as superior to the others (details below).
Circuit	Translation of the Greek *periodos*; the same as the Big Four.
Coubertin, Pierre de (1863–1937)	Founder of the International Olympic Committee and usually given credit for the first modern Olympics.
Diaulos	A foot race two lengths of the stadium, so that the runners finished where they started. It was about 400 meters (at Olympia, a little less).
Ekecheiria (Greek)	Literally, "Restraining the hands" or "Hands-off," the Olympic truce (see chapter 11).
Halteres (Greek)	Literally, "jumpers," the weights carried in each hand by Greek long jumpers (see chapter 3).
Himantes (Greek)	Strips of leather ("thongs") wrapped around the hands of boxers as a hand covering.
Hoplites (Greek)	"Armed Race." A foot race in which the athletes ran two lengths of the stadium while wearing armor.

IOC   "International Olympic Committee"; the group (which itself selects new members) that administers the international Olympic Games. It was founded by Pierre de Coubertin in 1894.

Keryx (Greek)   A "herald" or "announcer"; there was a contest for this post at the start of each Olympiad after 396 BC.

Magna Graecia (Latin)   That portion of Sicily and southern Italy which was inhabited mainly by Greeks in antiquity.

Palaestra (Greek)   Literally, "place to wrestle"; a building for wrestlers, pancratiasts, and boxers (see chapter 3).

Pancration (Greek)   "All forms of power," a kind of "all-in" fighting or "no-holds-barred" combative event, where almost all blows and tactics were legal (see chapter 4).

Periodonikes (Greek)   An athlete who had won in each of the Big Four or "Circuit" (*periodos*).

Salpinktes (Greek)   A trumpeter; there was a contest for this post at the start of each Olympiad after 396 BC. The trumpeter called the spectators to attention, and signaled parts of the equestrian events.

Stade (Greek)   A foot race one length of the stadium, equivalent to our 200 meter dash; at Olympia, the distance was 192.27 meters; some other stadiums were a little shorter, but a few were a little longer.

Tethrippon (Greek)   Contest for four horse chariots or one of those chariots.

Bibliography

Anderson, Graham, *Philostratus*, London and Sydney (Croom Helm), 1986.

Borgers, Walter, *Olympic Torch Relays, 1936–1994*, Kassel (Agon Sport-Verlag), 1996.

Brophy, R. H., Deaths in the Panhellenic Games I: Arrachion and Creugas, *American Journal of Philology* 99 (1978), 363–90; II. All Combative Sports, ibid, 106 (1985), 171–98.

Brundage, Avery, Why the Olympic Games? In: Asa Bushnell, ed., *Report of the United States Olympic Committee; Games of the XIVth Olympiad, London, England, 1948*, n.p. n.d. (New York, 1949?), United States Olympic Association, pp. 21–6.

Coubertin, Pierre de, Les Jeux Olympiques à Much Wenlock, *La Revue athlétique* 1 (December 1890), 705–13.

Coubertin, Pierre de, handwritten document, "Procès-verbal," in folder "Congrès 1894," IOC Archives, Lausanne.

Coubertin, Pierre de, *Batailles de l'éducation physique: Une campagne de vingt-et-un ans, 1887–1908*, Paris (Librairie de l'Éducation Physique), 1908.

Coubertin, Pierre de, *Mémoires Olympiques*, Paris, 1932.

Coubertin, Pierre de (Norbert Müller, ed.), *Textes Choisis*, 3 vols., Zurich (Weidmann), 1968.

Crowther, Nigel, Reflections on Greek Equestrian Events, *Nikephoros: Zeitschrift für Sport und Kultur im Altertum* 7 (1994), 121–33.

Dittenberger, Wilhelm, *Sylloge Inscriptionum Graecarum*, 3rd edn., 3 vols., Leipzig, 1915–24.

Drees, Ludwig, *Olympia*, New York (Praeger), 1968.

Ebert, Joachim, *Zum Pentathlon der Antike*, Abh. Der Akad. Wiss. zu Leipzig 56.1, Berlin (Akad.-Verlag), 1963.

Ebert, Joachim, *Griechische Epigramme auf Sieger an gymnischen und hippischen Agonen*, Berlin (Akad.-Verlag), 1972. (Citations are by inscription number; thus "Ebert 43" means inscription 43 not p. 43.)

Ebert, Joachim, Neues zum Hippodrom und zu den hippische Konkurrenzen in Olympia, *Nikephoros* 2 (1989), 89–108.

Ebert, Joachim, Die Beschriftete Bronzeplatte. In: Sinn 1995, pp. 238–41.

Finley, M. I. and Pleket, H. W. *The Olympic Games: The First Thousand Years*, New York (Viking), 1976.

Gardiner, E. N., Phayllos and his Record Jump, *Journal of Hellenic Studies* 24 (1904), 70–80.

Gardiner, E. N., *Greek Athletic Sports and Festivals*, London (Macmillan), 1910.

Gardiner, E. N., *Athletics of the Ancient World*, Oxford (Oxford University Press), 1930.

Glass, Steven, The Greek Gymnasium: Some Problems. In: Rashke, 2002, pp. 155–73.

Golden, Mark, *Sport and Society in Ancient Greece*, Cambridge (Cambridge University Press), 1998.

Guttmann, Allen, *From Ritual to Record*, New York (Columbia University Press), 1978.

Harris H. A., *Greek Athletes and Athletics*, London (Indiana University Press), 1967

Harris, H. A., *Sport in Greece and Rome*, Ithaca, NY (Cornell University Press), 1972.

Herrmann, F. G., Wrestling Metaphors in Plato's *Theaetetus*, *Nikephoros* 8 (1995), 77–109.

Kyle, Donald G., *Athletics in Ancient Athens*, Leiden (Brill), 1987.

Lämmer, Manfred, Der sogenannte Olympische Friede in der Griechischen Antike, *Stadion* 8–9 (1983), 47–70.

Langdon, Merle, Throwing the Discus in Antiquity, *Nikephoros* 3 (1990) 177–82.

Lee, Hugh, Women's Athletics and the Bikini Mosaic from Piazza Armerina, *Stadion* 10 (1984), 45–76.

Lee, Hugh, *The Program and Schedule of the Ancient Olympic Games*, Hildesheim (Weidmann), 2001.

Lennartz, Karl, *Kenntnisse und Vorstellung von Olympia und den Olympischen Spielen in der Zeit von 393–1896*, Schorndorf (Hofmann), 1974.

Lennartz, Karl, The 2nd International Olympic Games in Athens, 1906, *Journal of Olympic History* 10 (2001), 10–27.

Levi, Peter, *Pausanias: Guide to Greece*, 2 vols., Harmondsworth (Penguin Books), 1971.

Lewis, Charlton T. and Short, Charles, *A Latin Dictionary*, Oxford (Oxford University Press), 1958.

Poliakoff, Michael, *Combat Sports in the Ancient World*, New Haven, CT (Yale University Press), 1987.

Mahaffy, John, Old Greek Athletics, *MacMillan's Magazine* 36 (1879), 324–7.

Mallwitz, Alfred, Cult and Competition Locations at Olympia. In: Raschke 2002, pp. 79–109.

Miller, Stephen, *Arete*, 2nd edn., Berkeley (University of California Press), 1991.

Raschke, W. K., ed., *Archaeology of the Olympics*, 2nd edn., Madison (University of Wisconsin Press), 2002.

Roller, L. E., Funeral Games for Historical Persons, *Stadion* 7 (1981), 1–18.

Rudolph, W., Zu den Formen der Berufsport zur Seit des Poliskrise. In: Welskopf, E. C., ed., *Hellenische Poleis*, Berlin (Akad.-Verlag), 1974, vol 3, pp. 1472–83.

Scanlon, Thomas F., *Eros and Greek Athletics*, Oxford (Oxford University Press), 2002.

Shorey, Paul, Can We Revive the Olympic Games? *Forum* 19 (1895), 313–23.

Sinn, Ulrich, Bericht III, *Nikephoros* 7 (1994 [1995]), 229–50.

Sinn, Ulrich, *Olympia: Cult, Sport, and Ancient Festival*, Princeton, NJ (Markus Weiner), 2000.

Soutsos, Panagiotis, *Nekrikos dialogos kai ta ereipia tes palaias Spartes*, Athens, 1834.

Swaddling, Judith, *The Ancient Olympic Games*, London (British Museum Publications), 1980.

Sweet, Waldo, *Sport and Recreation in Ancient Greece*, Oxford (Oxford University Press), 1987.

Turner, Judy A., Greek Priesthoods. In: Michael Grant, ed., *Civilization of the Ancient Mediterranean II*, New York (Scribner's), 1988, pp. 925–32.

Valavanis, Panos, *Hysplex: The Starting Mechanism in Ancient Stadia*, translated by Stephen G. Miller, Berkeley (University of California Press), 1999.

Young, David C., *The Olympic Myth of Greek Amateur Athletics*, Chicago (Ares), 1984.

Young, David C., Athletics. In: Michael Grant, ed., *Civilization of the Ancient Mediterranean II*, New York (Scribner's), 1988, pp. 1131–42 (a very brief introduction to Greek athletics).

Young, David C., *The Modern Olympics: A Struggle for Revival*, Baltimore, MD (Johns Hopkins University Press), 1996.

Young, David C., First with the Most: Greek Athletic Records and "Specialization," *Nikephoros* 9 (1996 [1997]), 3–25.

Young, David C. and Bijkerk, Anthony Th., That Memorable First Marathon, *Journal of Olympic History* 7.1 (1999), 5–24.

Index